Becoming a Problem Solving Genius

A Handbook of Math Strategies

Edward Zaccaro

Hickory Grove Press

About the Author

Ed lives outside of Dubuque, Iowa, with his wife and three children. He has been involved in education in various forms since graduating from Oberlin College in 1974. Ed has taught students of all ages and abilities, but his focus for the past ten years has been working with mathematically gifted students at the elementary and middle school level. When unable to find sufficient curriculum and materials for his students, he began to develop his own, resulting in the following collection of books.

- ♦ *Primary Grade Challenge Math*
- ♦ *Challenge Math for the Elementary and Middle School Student*
- ♦ *Real World Algebra*
- ♦ *The Ten Things All Future Mathematicians and Scientists Must Know (But are Rarely Taught)*
- ♦ *Becoming a Problem Solving Genius*

Ed holds a Masters degree in gifted education from the University of Northern Iowa and has presented at state and national conferences in the areas of mathematics and gifted education.

Cover designed by Wilderness Graphics, Dubuque, Iowa.

Phone: 563-583-4767
E-mail: challengemath@aol.com
http://www.challengemath.com

Library of Congress Card Number: 2005939082
ISBN 10:   0-9679915-9-5
ISBN 13:   978-0-9679915-9-7

This book is dedicated to my students, whose passion for math and science is the reason that I teach.

Table of Contents

Think 1

Dan and four friends planned a 32-day hike to the summit of Mt. Everest. After they bought enough food to last the five people 32 days, three other friends decided that they also wanted to go along on the adventure. How long will the food last now that eight people are taking the trip?

Problems like these make your head start spinning because the brain has trouble knowing how to solve this type of problem.

How nice of you to notice! What can I do to make this problem easier to solve?

Because so many people cannot solve this type of problem, I have developed a problem solving method that makes these problems very easy.

It is called **Think 1.**

Think 1

In the problem about hiking to the top of Mt. Everest, ask yourself how long the food would last if only **one** person went on the trip.

Okay. If the food will last 5 people 32 days, it will last one person 5 x 32 = 160 days. That was easy!

Now it is easy to see that the food will last two people $160 \div 2 = 80$ days and three people $160 \div 3 = 53\frac{1}{3}$ days.

Now all you have to do is make a chart.

1 person...................160 days
2 people $(160 \div 2)$.....80 days
3 people $(160 \div 3)$.....53 1/3 days
4 people $(160 \div 4)$.....40 days
..
..
..
8 people $(160 \div 8)$.....20 days

That sure made the problem easy!

Try this problem using **Think 1**.

One bag of cat food will feed 3 cats for 40 days. If I buy 2 more cats, how long will one bag of cat food last?

You never told me you owned cats. I am very disappointed in you and I may not visit anymore!

Let's see, if one bag feeds **three** cats for 40 days, then one bag will feed **one** cat for 3 x 40 days = 120 days. Now I will make a chart.

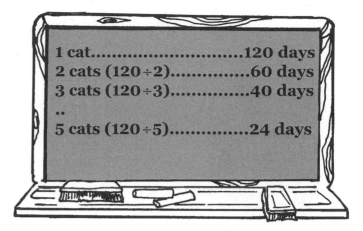

1 cat...........................120 days
2 cats (120÷2)...............60 days
3 cats (120÷3)...............40 days
..
5 cats (120÷5)...............24 days

Wasn't that easy! Now try one more to make sure you know how to use **Think 1**. By the way, my cats are scared of their own shadow, so don't worry about visiting.

Dave paints a fence in 4 hours while Sara paints the same fence in 2 hours. If they work together, how long will it take them to paint the fence?

Let's see, I will use **Think 1** by thinking about one hour.

Dave will paint $\frac{1}{4}$ of the fence in one hour and Sara will paint $\frac{1}{2}$ of the fence in one hour.

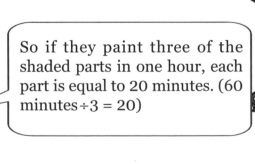

Together in one hour

That's right, so together they paint $\frac{3}{4}$ of the fence in one hour.

So if they paint three of the shaded parts in one hour, each part is equal to 20 minutes. (60 minutes ÷ 3 = 20)

Now it is clear that if Dave and Sara work together, it will take them one hour and 20 minutes to paint the fence.

Together in one hour

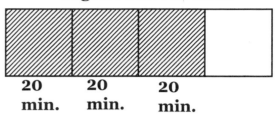

20 min.   20 min.   20 min.

I am ready for some hard problems now!

Level 1

1) It takes 5 workers 12 hours to unload one truck. How long would it take 6 workers to unload the truck?

2) After an explosion of an oxygen tank, three astronauts were forced to move into the lunar lander that was attached to their spacecraft.

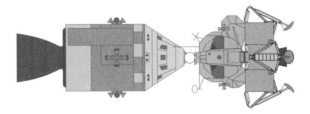

If the lunar lander had enough oxygen to last 2 people for 6 days, is there enough oxygen for 3 astronauts if their journey back to earth will take 4 days? Why or why not?

3) If it takes 3 people 4 hours to clean a warehouse, how long will it take 4 people to clean the warehouse?

4) If it takes 7 people 3 hours to dig a 50 cubic foot hole, how long will it take two people to dig the hole?

5) It takes Deanna 7 hours to paint a fence. What fraction of the fence does she paint in one hour?

Level 2

1) When Mike uses a riding mower, it takes him 3 hours to mow his lawn. When he uses a push mower, it takes him 6 hours to mow the lawn. (His sister also can mow the lawn with the push mower in 6 hours.)

Mike wanted to get the lawn mowed as quickly as possible, so he paid his sister $10 to mow with the push mower while he used the riding mower. How long will it take Mike and his sister to mow the lawn if they work together?

2) Luke and 5 friends packed enough food for a 2-week canoe trip. If one extra person decided to go on the trip at the last minute, how long will the food last?

3) If 12 workers can dig a tunnel in 100 days, how long will it take 20 workers to dig the tunnel?

4) A box of goldfish food can feed 3 fish for 4 weeks. How long will the box last if there are 7 goldfish?

5) Three people can pick all the apples from 5 trees in 5 hours. How long will it take 5 people to pick all the apples from the 5 trees?

Level 3

1) It takes a crew of 4 painters 12 hours to paint one house. If they wanted to paint the house in 8 hours, how many additional painters must they hire?

2) Hose A can fill a pool in 4 hours. Hose B can fill the pool in 2 hours. If both hoses are turned on at the same time, how long will it take to fill the pool?

3) Michelle can paint one car in 2 hours. It takes Tyler 3 hours to paint the same car while Colton takes 6 hours to paint the car. If they all work together, how long will it take them to paint the car?

4) Four children can eat a large pizza in 12 minutes. How long would it take 9 children to eat the same pizza? (Give your answer in minutes and seconds.)

5) When the water is turned on, a bathtub will be filled in 12 minutes. When the drain is opened it takes 20 minutes for the tub to drain. If the water is turned on and the drain is left open, how long until the tub is filled?

Einstein Level

1) When the drain is closed, a swimming pool can be filled in 4 hours. When the drain is opened, it takes 5 hours to empty the pool. The pool is being filled, but the drain was accidentally left open. How long until the pool is completely filled?

2) It takes 3 city snowplows 14 hours to clear 500 miles of road. If the city wants the 500 miles of road to be cleared in 6 hours, how many additional snowplows must they buy?

3) Brandon can shovel his sidewalk in 8 minutes, while his brother can shovel the walk in 12 minutes. If they work together, how long will it take them to shovel the sidewalk?

4) A construction crew must build a road in 10 months or they will be penalized $500,000. It took 10 workers 6 months to build half of the road. How many additional workers must be added to finish the road in the remaining 4 months?

5) Anna paints a fence in 4 hours while her brother paints it in 5 hours. If they work together, how long will it take them to paint the fence?

Super Einstein

Eight workers dug 3/8 of a tunnel in 10 days. If they need to finish the remaining 5/8 of the tunnel in $3\frac{1}{3}$ days, how many more workers must they hire?

The 2-10 Method

Luke was taking a math test to see how large a college scholarship he would receive. Most of the questions were easy, but one was very confusing.

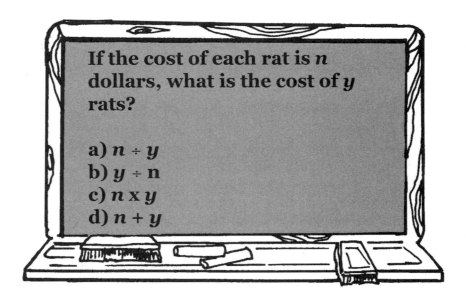

> **If the cost of each rat is _n_ dollars, what is the cost of _y_ rats?**
>
> a) _n_ ÷ _y_
> b) _y_ ÷ _n_
> c) _n_ x _y_
> d) _n_ + _y_

Luke had no idea how to do this problem until he remembered what Einstein told him a few months earlier.

Use the **2-10 Method** Luke. Use the **2-10 Method** Luke. Relax your mind and use the Use the **2-10 Method.**

The **2-10 Method** helps the brain understand how to solve difficult problems.

Plug in a 2 for the smaller number in a problem and a 10 for the larger number.

If the cost of each rat is 2 dollars, what is the cost of 10 rats?

In this problem we don't have numbers, we have letters taking the place of numbers, so I will plug in a 2 and a 10 where the letters are.

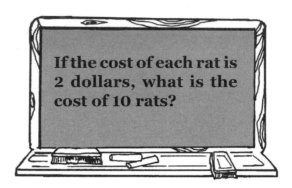

This problem is very easy to solve. I need to multiply: 2 x 10 = 20 dollars.

If the cost of each rat is 2 dollars, what is the cost of 10 rats?

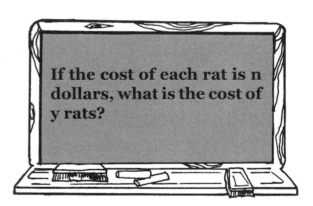

If the cost of each rat is n dollars, what is the cost of y rats?

Now I know the way to solve the problem is to multiply. The real problem is now easy to solve!

$$n \times y$$

The answer is *c) n x y*

Most people get the following problem wrong. Watch how easy it is when you use the **2-10 Method.**

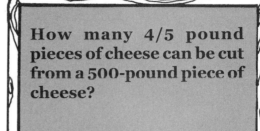

How many 4/5 pound pieces of cheese can be cut from a 500-pound piece of cheese?

My first thought is that the answer is 400, but I know that is wrong.

Use the **2-10 Method** and see how easy the problem really is!

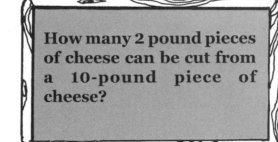

How many 2 pound pieces of cheese can be cut from a 10-pound piece of cheese?

That makes the problem very easy. The answer is obviously $10 \div 2 = 5$ pieces.

Now I know the way to solve the problem is by using division.

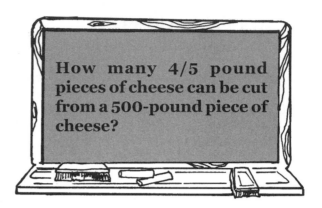

How many 4/5 pound pieces of cheese can be cut from a 500-pound piece of cheese?

I will now go back to the original problem and divide.

$$500 \div 4/5 = 625$$

Solve difficult problems with the **2-10 Method**!

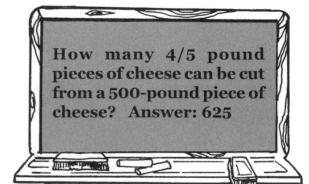

How many 4/5 pound pieces of cheese can be cut from a 500-pound piece of cheese? Answer: 625

Level 1

1) If $2\frac{1}{2}$ pounds of walnuts cost $2.50, how much do walnuts cost per pound?

2) If the price of cheese is $2.35 per pound, what is the cost of 2.45 pounds of cheese?

3) Kaartek bought 86 pizzas for a school party. If there are 516 people at his school, how much pizza should each person get?

4) If .75 inches on a map are equal to 6 miles, how many miles is one inch equal to?

5) There are y horses and z chickens in a barn. How many legs are there in the barn?

Level 2

1) How many 3/4 pound pieces can be cut from a giant 1200 pound meatball?

2) If Juan spent $1.28 for ground beef that cost $1.92 per pound, how much ground beef did Juan buy?

3) If the cost of each hat is x dollars, what is the cost of y hats?

4) If Jay reads $1\frac{1}{8}$ pages per minute, how long will it take him to read 72 pages?

5) A truck driver took 7 hours and 45 minutes to travel 426.25 miles. What was the average speed of the truck driver?

Level 3

1) A tank used 22 gallons of gas to go 17.6 miles. How many miles per gallon did the tank use?

2) Approximately 2800 red blood cells are created in the bone marrow each second. How many red blood cells would be created in .03125 seconds?

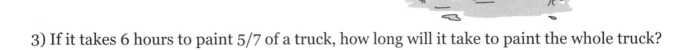

3) If it takes 6 hours to paint 5/7 of a truck, how long will it take to paint the whole truck?

4) The sound from a thunderstorm travels approximately 1/5 of a mile in one second. How far will sound travel in 18.6 seconds?

5) Lamar had N record albums that he tried to sell at a garage sale for $5 each. If the number of record albums he didn't sell is called Q, how much money did Lamar get from record album sales?

Einstein
Level

1) A 50-gallon water heater leaks .125 gallons of water every 14 minutes. How long until it is completely empty?

2) A spacecraft with a volume of 800 cubic feet is leaking air at a rate of .4 cubic feet every n minutes. How many minutes until the spacecraft has no air?

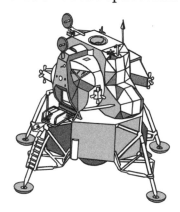

3) A meter is defined as the distance light travels in $1/299{,}792{,}458$ of a second. How many meters does light travel in 1/8 of a second?

4) Joseph can paint n cars in t hours. How long does it take Joseph to paint one car?

5) If a car is traveling at a speed of 60 miles per hour, how many hours will it take for the car to travel n miles?

Super Einstein

A gasoline tank is leaking at a rate of n gallons in t hours. If the gasoline cost \$2 per gallon, what is the value of the gasoline that will be lost in m minutes?

Sometimes You Must Subtract

Rachel decided to put carpet around the outside of her bedroom which was 24 feet long and 20 feet wide. If she wants the carpet to be 5 feet wide, how many square feet of carpet must Rachel buy?

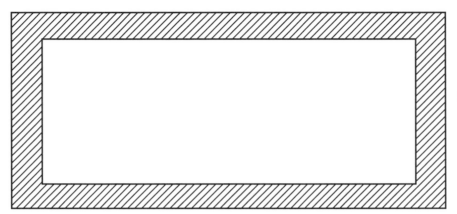

20 feet

24 feet

My first thought is to add up all the carpet pieces, but there must be an easier way.

You are right, there is an easier way to do this problem.

I see what I have to do next. I need to find the area of the inside part of the room.

24 feet

20 feet

24 feet

5'

14 feet

20 feet **5'** **10 feet** **5'**

5'

Because the carpet is 5 feet wide, I know the length of the inside of the room is 24 minus 5 minus another 5 = 14 feet.

And the width is 20 feet minus 5 minus another 5 = 10 feet.

The area of the inside is 10 feet x 14 feet = 140 square feet.

So the area of the carpet is 480 square feet minus 140 square feet = 340 square feet!

The power of **Somctimes You Must Subtract** is incredible. Look at this next problem.

Rachel came to a bridge that was crossing a deep canyon. A very strange cat was guarding the entrance to the bridge and when Rachel asked if she could cross the bridge, the cat said she must first answer a probability question.

"Your probability of crossing the bridge is n. What is your probability of not crossing the bridge?"

Use the power of...

Sorry, I went into a trance. Use **Sometimes You Must Subtract** and the question is very easy.

I know that if my probability of rolling a number cube and getting a "3" is $\frac{1}{6}$, then the probability of not rolling a "3" is $\frac{5}{6}$. I got that answer by subtracting: $1 - \frac{1}{6} = \frac{5}{6}$

Probabilities always add up to a whole or "1". If I know the probability of something happening, then it is easy to find the probability of it not happening! Does anyone know why my eyes are so big?

Flipping a coin and getting heads: $\frac{1}{2}$

NOT getting heads: $1 - \frac{1}{2} = \frac{1}{2}$

Rolling a number cube and getting a "6": $\frac{1}{6}$

NOT getting a "6": $1 - \frac{1}{6} = \frac{5}{6}$

Picking the ace of hearts from a deck of cards: $\dfrac{1}{52}$

NOT picking the ace of hearts: $1 - \dfrac{1}{52} = \dfrac{51}{52}$

Probability of crossing the bridge: n
Probability of **NOT** crossing the bridge: $1 - n$

Rachel used the power of **Sometimes you Must Subtract** to correctly answer the strange cat's question. Use its power to solve the following questions.

Level 1

1) What is the measurement of angle A?

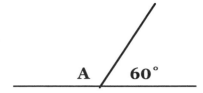

2) If two coins are flipped, what is the probability that there will not be two heads?

3) What is the measurement of angle P?

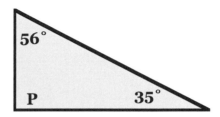

4) What is the area of the shaded part of the 5 by 10 rectangle shown below? (The white part is a one foot square.)

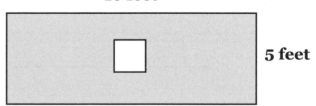

5) If the probability of getting struck by lightning each year is 1 in 1,000,000, what is the probability that you will not be struck by lightning in a year?

Level 2

1) Larry is rolling two dice. His dad told him that he can skip doing the dishes that night unless he rolls double sixes. What is the probability that Larry will be able to skip doing the dishes?

2) What is the area of the shaded figure?

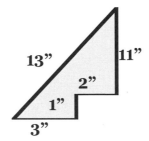

3) The regular price for a television is Q dollars. Each Saturday televisions are 20% off (the discount is .2Q). What is the price of a television on Saturday in terms of Q?

4) If the probability of winning is X, what is the probability of losing? (Assume there are no ties.)

5) The area of the square is 36 square inches. What is the area of the shaded part?

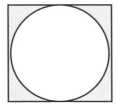

Level 3

1) Lines m and p are parallel. What is the value of x + y?

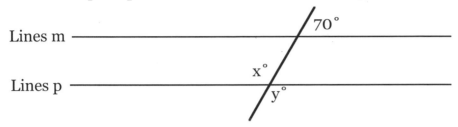

2) Fantasia decided to paint her circular room which had a diameter of 25 feet. She started painting in the center and when she had painted a circle with a 5-foot diameter, she used one quart of paint. How many more quarts of paint must Fantasia buy to finish her room?

3) Jonathan is going to carpet a 3 foot area around the border of his 20' by 24' room. How many square feet of carpeting must he buy?

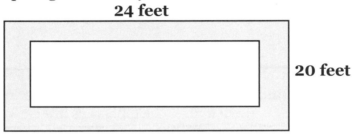

4) P is the center of the circle. The radius of the circle is 10 inches. What is the area of the shaded part?

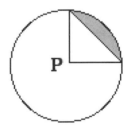

5) The area of the square is 100 square inches. Point A is the center of the square. What is the area of the shaded part?

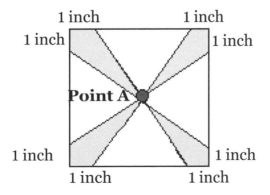

Einstein Level

1) It is known that 45% of men snore and 25% of women snore. A doctor looked at these numbers and made the following statement:

"If you put a man and a woman together, there is a 70% chance that someone is snoring." Explain why the doctor's math is wrong.

2) It is known that 45% of men snore and 25% of women snore. If you put a man and a woman together, what is the probability that someone will be snoring?

3) Keith is cutting two circular table tops out of a piece of plywood. The plywood is 4 feet by 8 feet and each table top has a diameter of 4 feet. If the price of a piece of plywood is $40, what is the value of the plywood that is wasted after the table tops are cut?

4) An eccentric millionaire decided to give away $1,000,000 if Janelle took one die and rolled a "4". He wanted Janelle to have a better than 1 in 6 chance of winning, so before she rolled the die he told her that she could roll the die 3 times. If any roll was a "4", she would win the million dollars. What are Janelle's chances of winning the million dollars?

5) Natalie made a deal with a farmer. She agreed to work for an entire year and in return, the farmer would give her $10,200 plus a prize pig.

After working for 5 months, Natalie decided to quit. The farmer determined that 5 months of work was equal to $3375 plus the pig. How much money was the pig worth?

Super Einstein

Two identical isosceles triangles are placed inside a 20" by 5" rectangle as shown below:

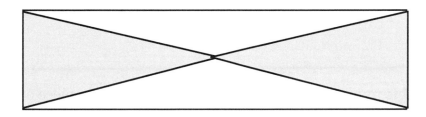

The length of the rectangle is then shortened to 15", forcing the triangles to overlap equally. What is the area of the overlapping part?

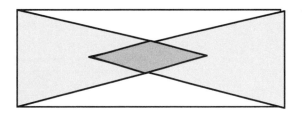

Draw a Picture

An eccentric mathematician visited Rachel's classroom and wrote a problem on the black board:

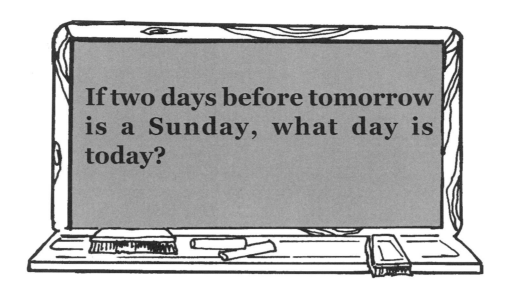

Several students in Rachel's class raised their hands to answer the question. The eccentric mathematician wrote all the answers the students gave on the board:

The problem seems easy, but my brain really starts to spin when I try to answer it.

Don't worry, Einstein has given me a problem solving method to share with you that will make the problem very easy!

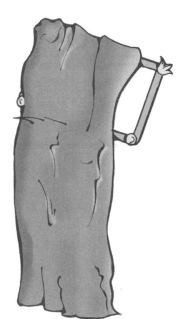

Has anyone ever seen this so-called eccentric mathematician and Einstein together at the same time? I am starting to get suspicious.

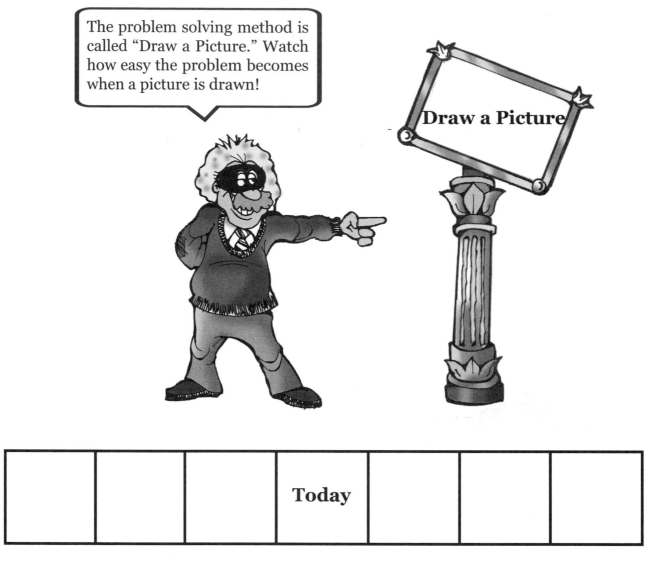

The problem solving method is called "Draw a Picture." Watch how easy the problem becomes when a picture is drawn!

Draw a Picture

			Today			

Step 1: Draw boxes that will be days of the week.

Step 2: Pick a box and call it today.

Step 3: Now we know where yesterday is. We also know where tomorrow is.
Let's write them down:

		Yesterday	Today	Tomorrow		

Step 4: The problem says that 2 days before tomorrow is a Sunday. Let's go back two days from tomorrow and write in Sunday:

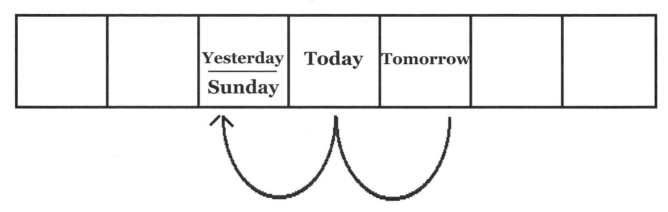

Step 5: Now it is easy to see that today is Monday.

Unbelievable! Drawing a picture made the problem very easy!

Before I leave, I have another problem that you can easily solve by drawing a picture.

The gas tank in my car was 3/8 full. After I put in 6 gallons of gas, the tank was 3/4 full. How large is the gas tank?

Level 1

1) Three days before the day after tomorrow is Monday. What day is today?

2) Eight gallons were poured into a gas tank that was 1/4 full. Now the tank is 3/4 full. How many gallons does a full tank hold?

3) A board must be cut into three pieces that are the same length. If it takes five minutes for each cut, how long will it take to saw the board into three pieces that are the same size?

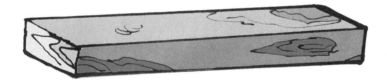

4) Rick is taller than Luke, who is taller than Bruce. Steve is taller than Bruce, but not as tall as Rick. If Luke is 6 feet tall, do we know if Steve is taller than 6 feet?

5) Maria leaves her house and runs west for 6 miles. She then turns north and runs 5 miles. Maria then travels east for 7 miles and then south for 5 miles. How far is Maria from her house now?

Level 2

1) Kris wants to fence in her square garden that is 40 feet on each side. If she places posts every 10 feet, how many posts will she need?

2) Jon earned money baby-sitting. He spent 1/4 of the money on a guitar and then he gave 1/4 of what was left to charity. If he has $108 left, how much money did he start with?

3) Sound takes 5 seconds to go one mile. Clark is standing near a rock wall and when he shouts, it takes 20 seconds for the echo to reach his ears. How far away is the rock wall?

4) A dog on a 20-foot long leash is tied to the middle of a fence that is 100 feet long. The dog ruined the grass wherever it could reach. What is the area of the grass that the dog ruined?

5) If sound travels 1/5 of a mile in one second, how many miles does it travel in 1/5 of a second?

Level 3

1) A gas tank is 1/4 full. When Raol puts 4 gallons of gasoline into the tank, it is 5/8 full. How many gallons does a full tank hold?

2) Four days before the day after tomorrow is a Wednesday. What day of the week was it 13 days before yesterday?

3) A rocket club launches rockets every 12 minutes. How many rockets will be launched in one hour?

4) A sprinkler that waters in a circular pattern shoots water to a distance of 15 feet. If the sprinkler is set in the middle of a 30 foot by 30 foot yard, how many square feet of the lawn does the sprinkler miss?

5) A rectangle has a width that is 1/8 its length. If the perimeter of the rectangle is 126 inches, what is the width of the rectangle?

Einstein Level

1) While exploring an undersea wreck, Nancy found a large bag of gold. She gave half of the gold to her mother and 1/4 to her father. Nancy then gave 1/3 of the remaining gold to her brother and 1/2 to her sister. Nancy then donated half of the gold that remained to charity. If Nancy now has 1.25 pounds of gold, how many pounds did she find?

2) Warren lived 60 miles from school. He traveled at an average speed of 45 miles per hour and arrived at school 15 minutes after the 8:00 starting time. What time did Warren leave his home?

3) Sara, Claudia, Karen and Kath are sisters who inherited money from an uncle. Claudia received 1/5 of the money while Karen received 1/2 of the money. Kath received 1/4 and Sara was given the rest. If Sara received $1750, how much money did all four sisters inherit?

4) A storage tank is completely empty. At 12:00 noon, oil is poured into the top of the tank and a valve is opened at the bottom. Oil is poured into the tank at a rate of 2.1 gallons per minute and the valve at the bottom empties the tank at a rate of 1.9 gallons per minute. If the tank does not fill until 12:00 noon the next day, how many gallons does the tank hold?

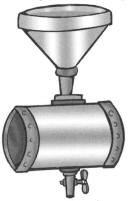

5) How many square feet of paint are needed to paint the outside of a cylindrically shaped gas tank that is resting on the ground? The diameter of the tank is 20 feet and it is 30 feet high. (Because the tank is resting on the ground, the bottom will not be painted.)

Super Einstein

A large square piece of paper is repeatedly folded in half. The first fold makes a rectangle and the next fold returns the shape to a square. This pattern is repeated until there are 13 folds. At this point, the area of the paper is $\frac{9}{32}$ of a square inch. What is the length of a side of the original square?

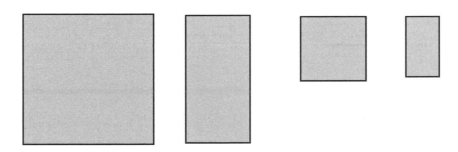

Venn Diagrams

Look at the problem on the blackboard. Without a special problem solving tool called Venn diagrams, the problem would be very confusing and almost impossible to solve.

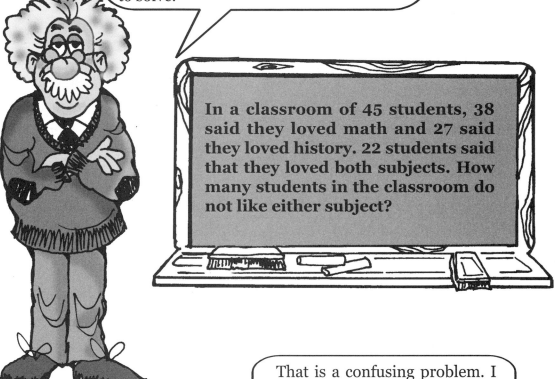

In a classroom of 45 students, 38 said they loved math and 27 said they loved history. 22 students said that they loved both subjects. How many students in the classroom do not like either subject?

That is a confusing problem. I think that I will draw a Venn diagram to help me solve it.

I will first draw two circles that stand for **I love math** and **I love history**. The shaded part that is part of both circles will contain students who love both subjects.

In a classroom of 45 students, 38 said they loved math and 27 said they loved history. 22 students said that they loved both subjects. How many students in the classroom do not like either subject?

I will put 22 in the shaded part because that area contains the students who loved both subjects. I will also put a circle and a question mark next to the Venn diagram. This is the circle that stands for students who did not like either subject.

I Love Math
Circle (38)

I Love History
Circle (27)

22

?

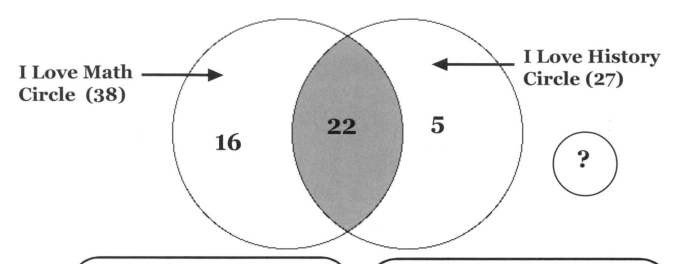

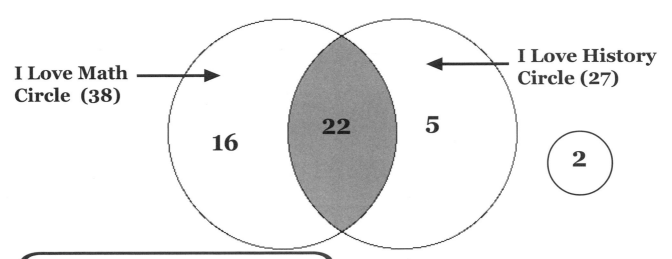

I Love Math Circle (38)

I Love History Circle (27)

16

22

5

2

I have 16 + 22 + 5 = 43 students in my Venn diagram, but there are 45 students in the classroom. Because of this I know that there must be 2 students in the circle outside the Venn diagram. Wow, that was fun!!

Did you know that Venn diagrams are named after John Venn, a mathematician who was born in 1834?

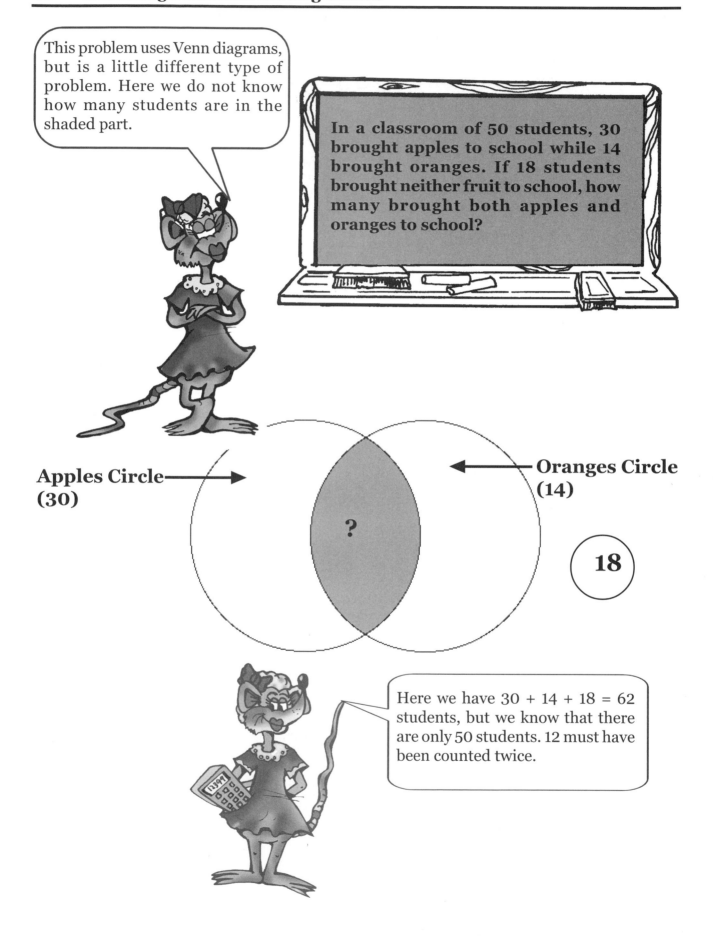

This problem uses Venn diagrams, but is a little different type of problem. Here we do not know how many students are in the shaded part.

In a classroom of 50 students, 30 brought apples to school while 14 brought oranges. If 18 students brought neither fruit to school, how many brought both apples and oranges to school?

Apples Circle (30)

Oranges Circle (14)

?

18

Here we have 30 + 14 + 18 = 62 students, but we know that there are only 50 students. 12 must have been counted twice.

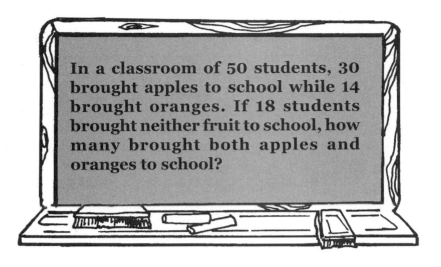

In a classroom of 50 students, 30 brought apples to school while 14 brought oranges. If 18 students brought neither fruit to school, how many brought both apples and oranges to school?

Apples Circle (30)

Oranges Circle (14)

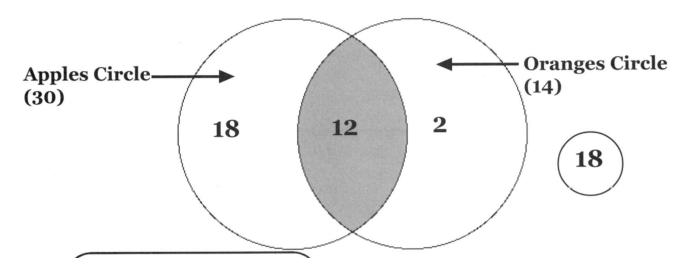

18   12   2

18

After I insert 12 students into the shaded area, I can finish the Venn diagram. 18 + 12 + 2 + 18 = 50. Venn diagrams come to the rescue again!!

Level 1

1) Place each item in its proper place in the Venn diagram:

Banana   **Strawberry**
Apple   **Stop Sign**
Orange   **Cardinal**

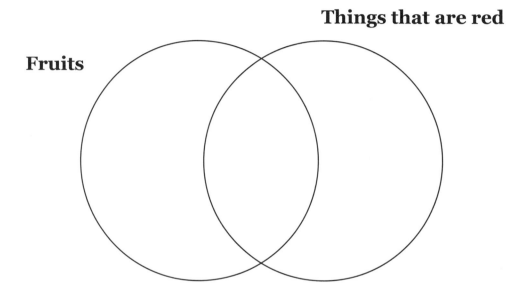

2) When a Venn Diagram is drawn showing Selena's pets and Devon's pets, what animals are in the shaded part?

Selena's pets: fish, cat, ferret, dog, horse, raccoon
Devon's pets: cat, guinea pig, dog, rat

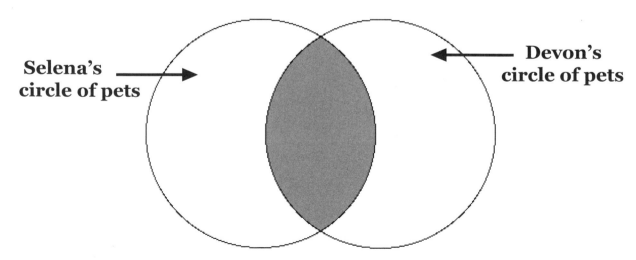

3) A class was asked about their favorite football team. Eighteen students liked the Chicago Bears, 19 liked the Green Bay Packers, and 5 students liked both teams. How many students are in the class?

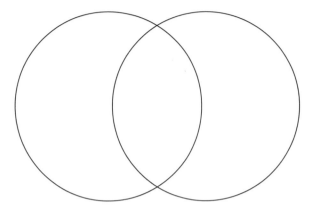

4) A soccer team has 18 players who kick with their right foot, 5 who kick with their left foot, and 2 who use both feet. How many players are on the team?

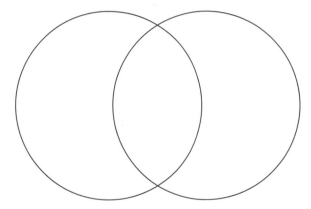

5) In Natalie's class, 18 children listed math as their favorite subject while 15 said English was their favorite subject. Eleven children liked both subjects equally well and 3 children didn't like either math or English. How many children are in the class?

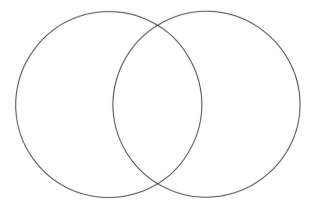

Level 2

1) In a classroom of 48 children, 25 like mushroom pizza while 32 like sausage. If 15 children like both mushroom and sausage, how many children in the classroom do not like either topping?

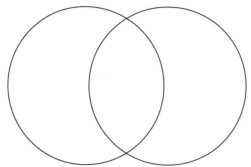

2) There are 48 dogs at the pound. Of these dogs, 11 have fleas, 6 have worms and 3 have both worms and fleas. How many dogs at the pound have neither worms nor fleas?

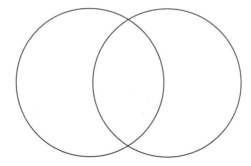

3) One hundred people were sent a questionnaire asking whether they had a cat or a dog as a pet. 28 people answered the questionnaire.

    Dog: 5
    Cat: 13
    Both: 3
    Neither: ?

How many people who answered the questionnaire did not have a dog or a cat for a pet?

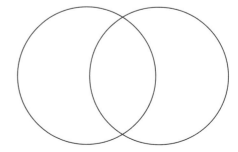

4) Look at the list of pets that Jared, Tyler and Austin own and then decide which animals belong in the shaded area?

Jared's pets: frog, dog, cat, fish, rat, pig
Tyler's pets: rat, ferret, fish
Austin's pets: fish, snake, rat, pig, parrot

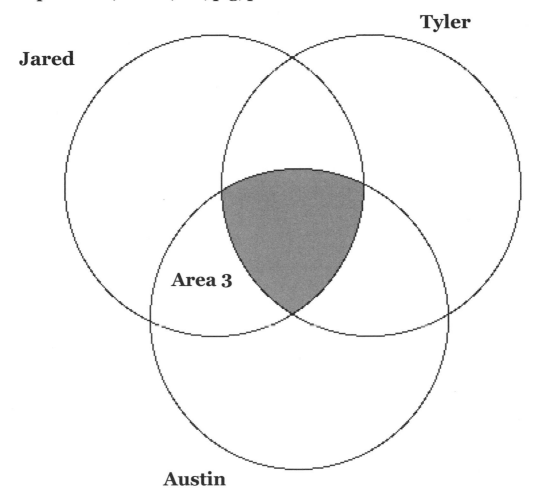

5) Look at the Venn Diagram from question number 4. Which animal belongs in the area marked area 3?

Level 3

1) What type of quadrilateral is in the shaded area?

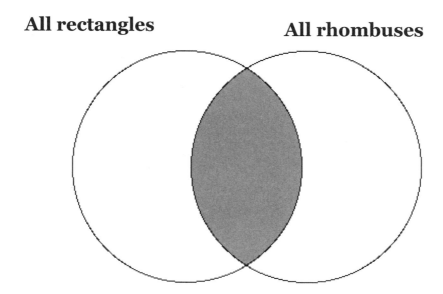

All rectangles   **All rhombuses**

2) Match A, B, and C with the following.

Scalene Triangles
Isosceles Triangles
Equilateral Triangles

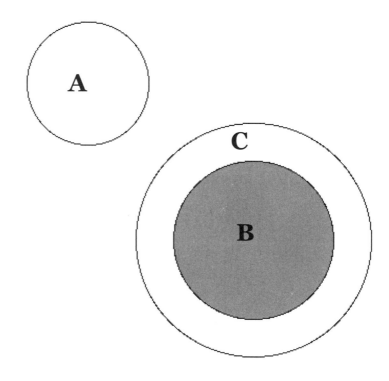

3) What numbers should be placed in the shaded area?

All prime numbers less than 20   **Odd numbers less than 40**

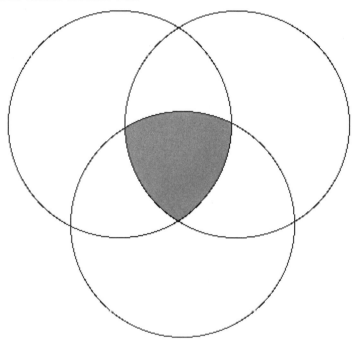

Integers greater than 0 and less than 20

4) Place the following animals in the proper space in the Venn diagram below:

Fish	**Geese**	**Porpoises**	**Wild Turkeys**
Alligator	**Robins**	**Killer whales**	**Frogs**
Crocodile	**Cats**	**Seals**	**Toads**
Ducks	**Dogs**	**Penguins**	**Sea Lions**

Hint: Space A plus the shaded part is for animals that can fly and also live in or on water. The shaded part is for those animals that do all three. (Animals that do all three also include the animals that fly and also live in or on water.) The white part (Space A) is for those that can fly and also live in or on water, but do not live or travel on land.

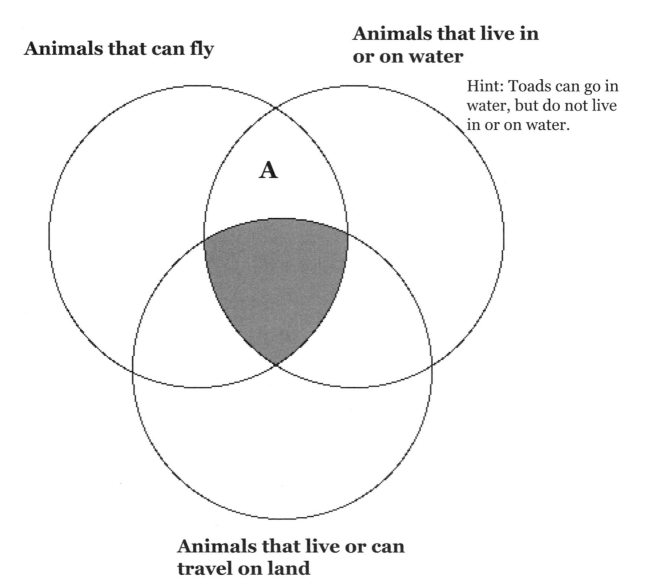

Animals that can fly

Animals that live in or on water

Hint: Toads can go in water, but do not live in or on water.

A

Animals that live or can travel on land

5) A survey was conducted in a city to see why so many businesses were failing. Fill in the Venn diagram using the results given below:

42 businesses failed due to a bad location.
13 businesses failed due to poor customer service.
9 businesses failed due to a rodent infestation.
7 businesses failed because of poor service and a rodent infestation.
4 businesses failed because of a bad location and a rodent infestation.
9 businesses failed because of a bad location and poor customer service.
3 businesses failed because of all three reasons.

Hint: Space B plus the shaded part is for businesses that failed because of a bad location and poor customer service. The shaded part is for businesses that failed for all three reasons. The white part is for businesses that failed because of a bad location and poor customer service but not rodents.

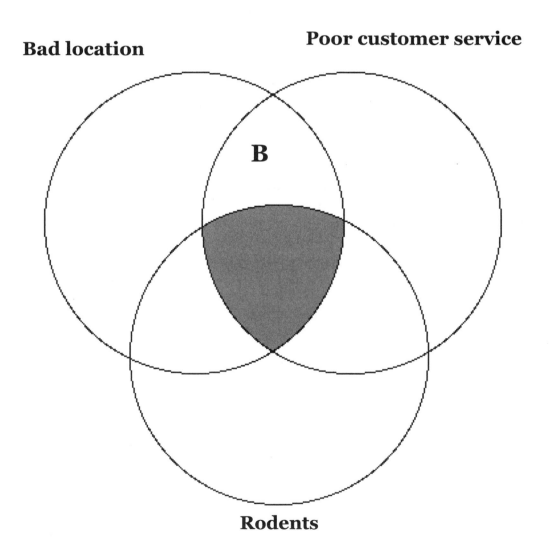

Einstein Level

1) Look at the information below and then determine
how many dogs there are at the animal shelter.

17 dogs at the animal shelter had no parasites.
10 dogs had fleas
9 had worms
8 had ticks.
2 dogs had fleas and ticks
4 had worms and fleas
4 dogs had ticks and worms.
1 poor dog had all three.

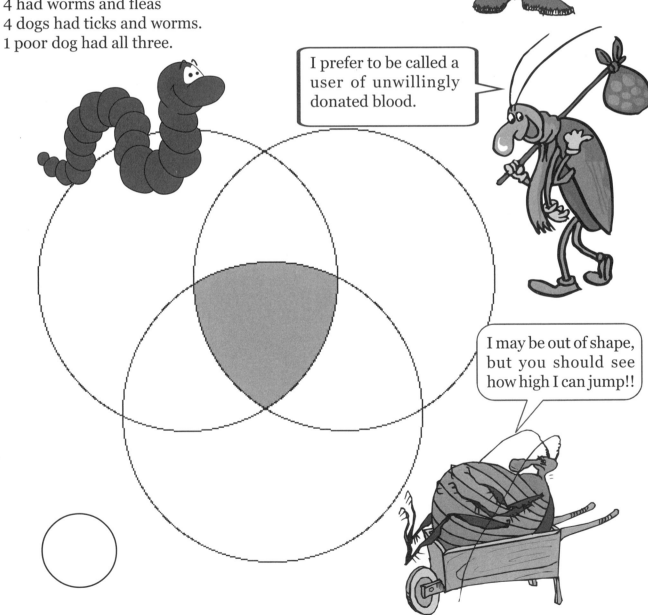

I prefer to be called a
user of unwillingly
donated blood.

I may be out of shape,
but you should see
how high I can jump!!

2) A Christmas vacation assignment for an English class of 30 students was to read the following three novels:

1) Wuthering Heights
2) Jane Eyre
3) Great Expectations

When vacation was over, the teacher found out that not very many students had completed the assignment.

14 read Jane Eyre
12 read Wuthering Heights
10 read Great Expectations
3 read all three books
8 read Jane Eyre and Wuthering Heights
5 read Jane Eyre and Great Expectations
6 read Great Expectations and Wuthering Heights

How many students did not read any of the books?

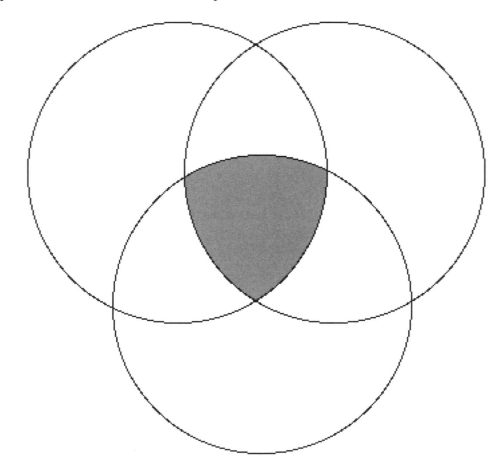

3) A classroom was asked to vote on what color they wanted for their school flag. The choices were blue, red and green. Eight children voted for red, 15 voted for green, and 11 picked blue. Three children voted for red and green, while 2 children voted for blue and red. Six children voted for blue and green and 1 child voted for all three colors. Six students didn't like any of the colors. How many children were in the classroom?

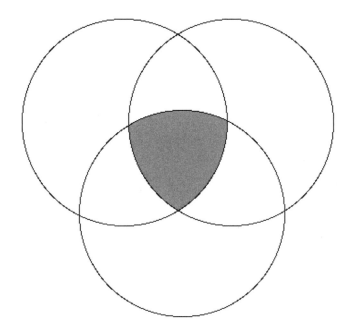

4) Students in a Spanish club visited several countries over summer vacation. Eleven traveled to Spain, while 19 visited Costa Rica and 24 traveled to Mexico. Five students visited Costa Rica and Spain while 6 students traveled to Costa Rica and Mexico. Eight students went to both Spain and Mexico, and 4 students went to all three countries. If there were 47 students in the Spanish club, how many didn't go to any of the three countries?

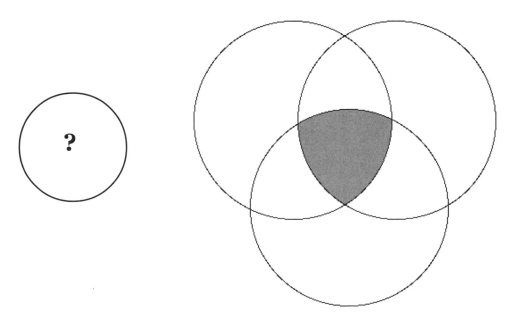

5) In the 1950's, most children caught diseases that children no longer get today. In the 1950's, 75 children were asked if they had ever had measles, German measles, or the whooping cough. Below you will find the results of the survey:

Measles: 46 children
Whooping cough: 31 children
German measles: 45 children
German measles and measles: 25 children
Whooping cough and measles: 24
Whooping cough and German measles: 22
None of the three diseases: 8
All three diseases: ?????

How many of the 75 children had all three diseases?
Hint: Call the missing part n.

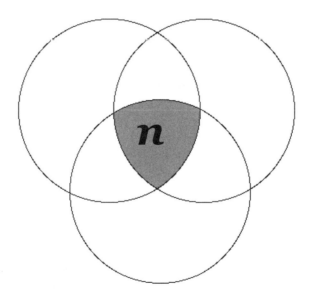

Super Einstein

Place each geometric figure in its proper place:

Polygons
Quadrilaterals
Parallelograms
Rhombuses
Squares
Rectangles
Trapezoids
Triangles
Equilateral triangles
Isosceles triangles
Scalene triangles

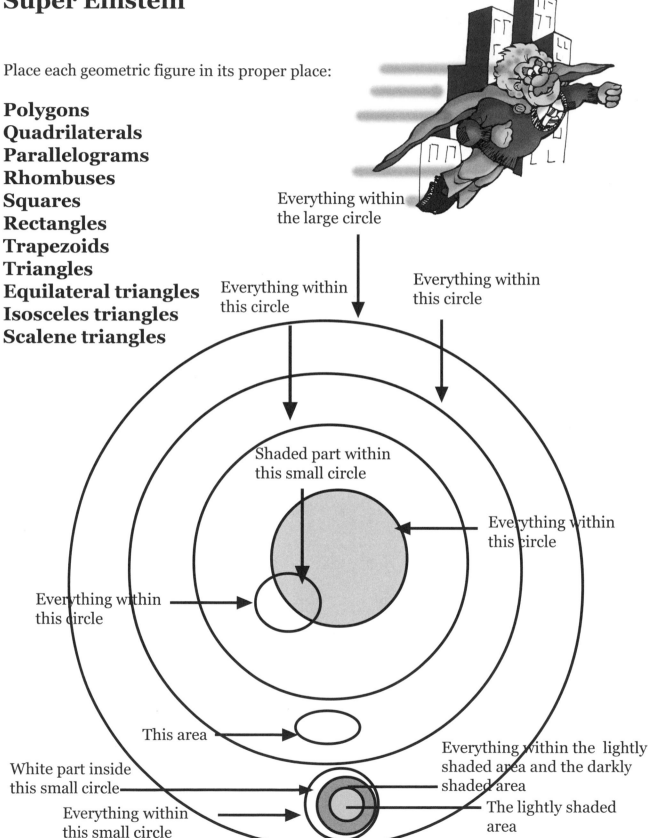

Everything within the large circle

Everything within this circle

Everything within this circle

Shaded part within this small circle

Everything within this circle

Everything within this circle

This area

White part inside this small circle

Everything within this small circle

Everything within the lightly shaded area and the darkly shaded area

The lightly shaded area

Language of Algebra

Before you visit a foreign country, it is very helpful to learn the language of the country you are visiting. You are about to enter the world of algebra. Before your visit however, it is very important that you learn the language of algebra.

You will be surprised at how easy algebra really is when you learn the math language of algebra.

Let's say you don't know how many cats there are in this pet store.

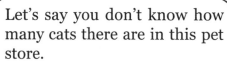

I know. Let's call the number of cats "**?**".

We could call the number of cats "**?**", but we want to talk in the language of algebra so we will use a letter instead of a question mark. Let's call the number of cats **n**.

Number of cats: *n*
Cat legs:
Cat eyes:
Cat tails:

Now we can translate cat legs, eyes, and tails into the language of algebra. This is almost as fun as eating cheese!

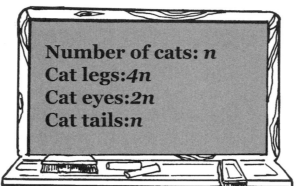

If we had 5 cats, we would have 5 x 4 = 20 legs. If we had *n* cats, we would have *n* x 4 = 4*n* legs.

We can use that same thinking to turn the eyes and tails into the language of algebra.

Number of cats: *n*
Cat legs: *4n*
Cat eyes: *2n*
Cat tails: *n*

I have an unknown number of mice in this box. I am going to translate some information into the language of algebra.

Number of mice: *n*
Number of mouse eyes: 2*n*
Number of mouse legs: 4*n*
Number of mouse toes: 20*n*
Number of mouse lungs: 2*n*

Let's try a translation into the math language of algebra that is a little more difficult.

This container is filled with **n** gallons of water.

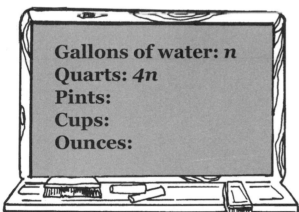

Gallons of water: *n*
Quarts: *4n*
Pints:
Cups:
Ounces:

I know that there are 4 quarts in each gallon. If there are *n* gallons, then there are *n* x 4 = 4*n* quarts.

See if you can change pints, cups and ounces into the math language of algebra.

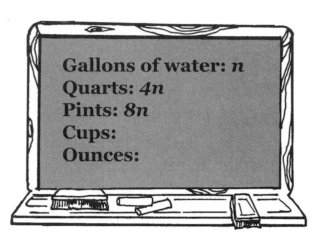

Gallons of water: n
Quarts: $4n$
Pints: $8n$
Cups:
Ounces:

I know that there are 2 pints in each quart. If there are $4n$ quarts, then there are $4n \times 2 = 8n$ pints.

I know that there are 2 cups in each pint. Because there are $8n$ pints, there must be $2 \times 8n = 16n$ cups. Now I know there are $8 \times 16n = 128n$ ounces because there are 8 ounces in each cup.

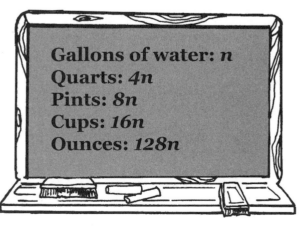

Gallons of water: n
Quarts: $4n$
Pints: $8n$
Cups: $16n$
Ounces: $128n$

There is a trick that will help your brain translate into the math language of algebra.

If you want to change n feet into yards in the math language of algebra, ask yourself how you would change 60 feet into yards. The answer of course is $60 \div 3 = 20$ yards.

I can't believe how easy the problem is now!!! All I have to do is do the same thing to n that I did to 60!

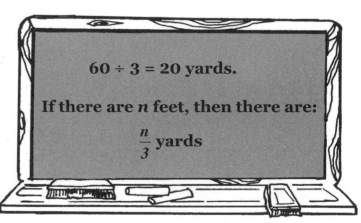

$60 \div 3 = 20$ **yards.**

If there are n feet, then there are:

$$\frac{n}{3} \text{ yards}$$

Level 1

1) If a rock rolled n meters,
how many decimeters did it roll?

Did you know that there are 10 decimeters in one meter?

2) Daniel's gas tank holds n gallons of gas.
How many pints does the tank hold?

Did you know that there are 4 quarts in a gallon and 2 pints in each quart?

3) If there are n days in a vacation, how many hours are there in the vacation?

4) Janey is n feet tall. How many inches tall is she?

5) In the year 1989, Luke's age was 3 times Rachel's age and Rachel's age was 3 times Dan's age. If Dan's age was n, how old were Rachel and Luke?

Dan's age: n
Rachel's age:
Luke's age:

6) If Enika walked *n* yards, how many feet did she walk?

Language of algebra:

Distance Enika walked in yards: *n*
Distance Enika walked in feet:

7) What is the value of an unknown number of nickels expressed in cents?

Language of algebra:

Number of nickels: *n*
Value of the nickels:

8) William is traveling at a speed of 50 miles per hour. How far will William travel in *n* hours?

Language of algebra:

Speed: 50 miles each hour
Time: *n* hours
Distance:

Did you know that you can find the circumference of any circle by multiplying the diameter by pi (3.14)?

9) If the diameter of a circle is *n*, what is the circumference

Language of algebra:

Diameter: *n*
Circumference:

10) There are five consecutive numbers and the smallest is called *n*. What is the largest number called?

Largest:
Next:
Next:
Next:
Smallest: *n*

Level 2

1) If a soccer ball was kicked a distance of *n* decimeters, how many meters did it travel?

Language of algebra:

Decimeters: *n*
Meters:

2) If Colton ran *n* kilometers, how many millimeters did he run?

Language of algebra:

Kilometers: *n*
Millimeters:

Did you know that there are 1000 millimeters in a meter and 1000 meters in each kilometer?

3) What is the sum of four consecutive multiples of 5? (Call the smallest number *n*.)

Language of algebra:

Largest:
Next:
Next:
Smallest: *n*

4) Nolan is paid $9 per hour plus a bonus of $55 per week.
If Nolan worked *n* hours during a week, how much was he paid?

Language of algebra:

Hours worked: *n*
Pay for the week:

5) Amelda had *n* shoes in her closet. How many pairs of shoes did she have?

Language of algebra:

Shoes: *n*
Pairs of shoes:

6) The regular cost of a guitar is *n*. On Saturdays all guitars are 15% off. What is the price of the guitar on Saturday?

Language of algebra:

Regular price: *n*
Saturday's price:

7) What is the value of *n* quarters expressed as dollars?

Language of algebra:

Number of quarters: *n*
Value of the quarters in dollars:

8) Sara earns $6000 more than 1/3 of Claudia's yearly salary. If Claudia's salary is *n*, what is Sara's salary?

Language of algebra:

Claudia's salary: *n*
Sara's salary:

9) A desk and a chair together cost $1550. If the cost of the chair is *n*, what is the cost of the desk?

Language of algebra:

Chair: *n*
Desk:

10) If angle #2 has a measurement of *n*°, what is the measure of angle #1?

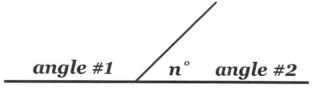

angle #1   *n*°   *angle #2*

Level 3

1) Joe talked for n seconds. How many hours did Joe talk?

Language of algebra:

Time Joe talked in seconds: n
Time Joe talked in hours:

2) Julio had a coin box that consisted of only quarters and dimes. The number of quarters was three times the number of dimes. If the number of dimes is n, what is the value of the coins in the coin box?

Language of algebra:

Number of dimes: n Value of dimes:
Number of quarters: Value of the quarters:

Value of the coin box:

3) What is the measure of the remaining angle in the trapezoid shown below?

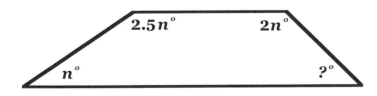

4) If a snail crawled n millimeters, how many kilometers did it travel?

Language of algebra:

Millimeters: n
Kilometers:

I hope you remembered that there are 1000 millimeters in a meter and 1000 meters in each kilometer.

5) Dennis drank *n* pints of water during a marathon.
How many gallons of water did he drink?

6) The distance along the circle from point A to point B
is *n* inches. What is the distance from point B to point A if you
travel along the circumference and go through point C?

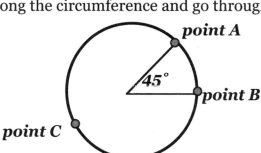

point A

45°

point B

point C

7) Aaron bought a guitar for *n* dollars. The tax in his state is 6%. What is the total cost of the
guitar including tax?

Language of algebra:
Guitar: *n*
Tax:
Total:

8) A rectangle has a length that is 8.5 times its width. If the width is *n*, what is the perimeter of
the rectangle?

Language of algebra:
Width: *n*
Length:
Perimeter:

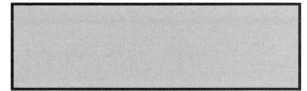

9) Deanna has 5-cent stamps and 10-cent stamps. If she has 100 total stamps, what is the
value of the stamps? (Call the number of 5-cent stamps *n*.)

Language of algebra:
Number of 5-cent stamps: *n*   Value of 5-cent stamps:
Number of 10-cent stamps: Value of 10-cent stamps:

10) There are cows and chickens in a barn along with a three-legged
dog named Tripod. If there are twice as many chickens as cows,
how many legs are there in the barn? (Call the number of cows *n*.)

Number of cows: *n*   Number of cow legs:
Number of chickens: Number of chicken legs:
Tripod's legs: 3

Einstein Level

1) Luke drove for *n* hours at 55 miles per hour. Luke's mother drove for *n* hours at a speed of 60 miles per hour. How much farther than Luke did his mother drive?

Language of algebra:

Distance Luke drove:
Distance Mom drove:

2) There are only horses and ducks on a farm. There are 80 animals in all and the number of ducks is called *n*. How many horse legs are there on the farm?

Language of algebra:

Number of ducks: Number of duck legs:
Number of horses: Number of horse legs:

3) Stuart traveled *n* miles at a speed of 72 miles per hour. How many seconds did it take for Stuart to travel the *n* miles?

Language of algebra:

Speed: 72 mph
Distance: *n* miles
Time:

Did you know that
Distance = Speed x Time?

4) A garden has a length that is three times its width. If the width is *n* feet and fencing cost $8 per foot, what is the cost of the fencing for the garden?

Language of algebra:

Width: *n*
Length:
Perimeter:
Cost of fencing:

5) A guitar that normally cost *n* dollars is on sale for 20% off. The tax is 8%.

What is the total cost of the guitar including tax?

Regular price of the guitar: *n*
Discount:
Discounted price:
Tax:
Total cost:

6) In terms of *n*, what is the total measure of angles A + B?

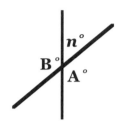

7) A farmer has a total of 200 ducks and cows in his barn. If he has *n* cows, how many total legs are there in the barn? (Make sure you include the farmer.)

Language of algebra:

Cows: *n*   Cow legs:
Ducks: Duck legs:
Farmer's legs: 2

8) What is the average of 7 consecutive numbers if the smallest number is called *n*?

Language of algebra:

Largest number:
Next:
Next:
Next:
Next:
Next:
Smallest number: *n*

9) Jacob bought a car that loses 10% of its value each year. If the original cost of the car is *n* dollars, what is its value after 3 years?

Language of algebra:

Value new: *n*
Value after 1 year:
Value after 2 years:
Value after 3 years:

10) The length of each side of the square is *n*. What is the area of the shaded part of the drawing?

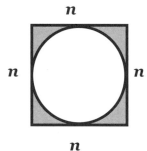

Did you know that the formula for the area of a circle is

$Area = \pi r^2$?

n

n   *n*

n

Super Einstein

A student was trying to determine a formula for changing speeds that are written in feet per second into miles per hour. If a sprinter runs at a speed of *n* feet per second, what is her speed in miles per hour?

Language of algebra:

Speed: *n* feet per second
Speed in miles per hour:

Solving Equations

When I first learned algebra from my grandmother, I made a terrible mistake that I have never forgotten. One of the most important rules of algebra is that you can do whatever you want to one side of an equation as long as you are fair and do the same thing to the other side of the equation. In a moment of carelessness, I forgot this rule.

> You can do whatever you want to one side of an equation as long as you are fair and do the same thing to the other side of the equation.

The equation I was working with was fairly simple: $n - 12 = 36$. I wanted the n to be all alone on one side of the equation so I added 12 to the left side of the equation. Now the n was all alone because $-12 + 12 = 0$. Unfortunately, in my hurry to solve the equation, I forgot the most important algebra rule and forgot to also add 12 to the right side of the equation. As you probably guessed, the result was horrendous. Not only did the equation get unbalanced and tip over, but the right side of the equation was so upset about the unfairness of my action that it started to cry uncontrollably.

> I knew you liked the left side more than my side!

$$n - 12 + 12 = 36$$

It took that equation a long time to forgive me for that mistake, but I am happy to report that for the last 60 years I have always been fair to both sides of every equation I work with. So my advice to you is please be fair to both sides of an equation. Feel free to do whatever you want to one side of an equation to help you solve it, but remember to also do exactly the same thing to the other side. I don't want another equation to go through the pain of what I did 20 years ago.

When we turn problems into algebra, we now know that it is almost like we are changing the words into a different language.

I started the day with $85. After I found a bag of money, I had $143. How much money was in the bag?

Since I know how to speak Algebra, I can turn your problem into the math language of Algebra. $85 plus some number equals $143. I could write that as an equation: $85 + n = 143$

Before we learn how to turn problems into equations, we need to know how to solve equations. To solve algebraic equations, you must go through four steps. The first step is called **collecting**. When we collect, we gather together things that are the same. Look at the following equation:

$5n + 3n + 25 + 10 + 5 = 2n + 3n + 60 + 13$

$$5n + 3n + 25 + 10 + 5 = 2n + 3n + 60 + 13$$

I can collect the n's because they are the same. $5n + 3n = 8n$ and $2n + 3n = 5n$

You can also collect the 25 and 10 and the 5 because they are the same thing. (They are numbers.) You can also collect 60 and $13 = 73$

When you collect, only collect on each side of the equation. We collected the n's on the left side and wrote down $8n$ and then collected the n's on the right side and wrote down $5n$.

The new equation becomes:
$$8n + 40 = 5n + 73$$

$$8n + 40 = 5n + 73$$

Before you go on to the next step, try collecting things that are alike in the equations below.

1) $8n + 6 + 2n = 16$

2) $19n + 6 - 5n + 7 = 55$

3) $-5n + 10n = -5 + 20$

4) $10n - 9n - 8 - 5 = 0$

5) $2n + 2n + 2n + 10 - 2 - 2 - 2 = 64$

Here are the answers. I hope you didn't have any trouble!

1) $10n + 6 = 16$

2) $14n + 13 = 55$

3) $5n = 15$

4) $n - 13 = 0$

5) $6n + 4 = 64$

The second step is called **Getting the n's all on one side of the equation.**

$$8n + 40 = 5n + 73$$
$$-5n \qquad\quad -5n$$
$$3n + 40 = \; 0 \; + 73$$

To get the n's on one side of the equation we will subtract $5n$ from both sides.

I understand now. You just used the fairness rule and subtracted $5n$ from both sides of the equation and the $5n$ disappeared from the right side.

$$3n + 40 = 73$$

Before you go on to the next step, practice getting the *n*'s on one side of the equation.

1) **2n = n + 13**

2) **5n - 2 + 2n = 2n + 3**

3) **n = 10 - n**

4) **8 + 2n = 3n + 4**

5) **16n = 15n + 5**

Here are the answers. I hope you didn't have any trouble making *n*'s disappear from one side.

1) 2n = n + 13
       -n   -n
       n = 13

2) 5n - 2 + 2n = 2n + 3
Collect: 7n - 2 = 2n + 3
            -2n   -2n
            5n - 2 = 3

3) n = 10 - n
   +n   +n
    2n = 10

4) 8 + 2n = 3n + 4
        -2n -2n
      8 = n + 4

5) 16n = 15n + 5
   -15n = -15n
      n = 5

You always want all the *n*'s to be on one side of the equation. When you are trying to decide what *n*'s to get rid of, it is less messy if you always remove the smaller one.

In this equation, if you had to choose between $2n$ and $7n$, you would want to subtract $2n$ from both sides of the equation.

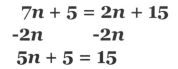

$$7n + 5 = 2n + 15$$
$$\underline{-2n \qquad\quad -2n}$$
$$5n + 5 = 15$$

In this equation, if you had to choose between $4n$ and $-7n$, you would want to add $7n$ to both sides of the equation to get rid of the $-7n$.

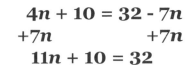

$$4n + 10 = 32 - 7n$$
$$\underline{+7n \qquad\qquad +7n}$$
$$11n + 10 = 32$$

The third step is called **Getting the *n*'s all by themselves.** The *n*'s do not want anything else on their side of the equation.

If you look at this equation, the 8*n* do not want the 11 to be with them on their side of the equation.

$$8n + 11 = 35$$

I don't know why the *n*'s want to be alone on their side of the equation. There is a rumor going around that *n*'s are antisocial and that is why they want to be alone.

Well anyway, whatever the reason, we can get the *n*'s all alone by subtracting 11 from both sides of the equation.

$$8n + 11 = 35$$
$$ -11 \quad -11$$
$$8n = 24$$

Sometimes I get equations like this. If I subtract 10 from both sides, it doesn't get rid of the -10 but turns it into -20. What should I do?

$$5n - 10 = 90$$
$$-10 \quad -10$$

That type of problem is really easy. All you need to do is add 10 to both sides and the negative number will disappear because -10 + 10 = 0.

$$5n - 10 = 90$$
$$+10 \quad +10$$
$$5n = 100$$

I'm glad you cleared that up. I was getting stressed out thinking about it. Try some equations on the next page and see if you can get the *n*'s all by themselves.

Maybe I'll build a fenced-in area and the *n*'s can stay in there all alone.

1) 7*n* + 3 = 17

2) 5*n* - 7 = 23

3) 20*n* - 7 - 7 = 66

4) 5 + *n* - 10 = 14

5) 7*n* - 5*n* - 3*n* + 2*n* + 11 = 44

Here are the answers. Good luck!

1) 7n + 3 = 17
　　　 -3　 -3
　　7n = 14

2) 5n - 7 = 23
　　　 +7　 +7
　　5n = 30

3) 20n - 7 - 7 = 66
　　　　　 +14 +14
　　20n = 80

4) 5 + n - 10 = 14
　　n - 5 = 14 (Collect)
　　　 +5　 +5
　　n = 19

5) 7n - 5n - 3n + 2n + 11 = 44
　　n + 11 = 44 (Collect)
　　　 - 11　 - 11
　　n = 33

The fourth step is called **Just one *n*.** We don't want 8*n*, we don't want 5*n*, we don't want 100*n*. We always want to have just one *n* or *n*.

Look at this equation. To turn the 8*n* into only 1*n*, we simply divide both sides by 8. 8*n* ÷ 8 is 1*n* or just *n*. 24 ÷ 8 = 3   Now we know that *n* = 3

$$8n = 24$$

$$\frac{8n}{8} = \frac{24}{8} \qquad n = 3$$

I know that the 8 caused us a problem, but why can't we just subtract the 8?

Anytime you have a number next to *n* you must divide to get rid of it. You can never just subtract it. Remember that 8*n* means 8 x *n*.

You will need to do the same thing to both sides of the equations to end up with only one *n*. May the force be with you.

1) $2n = 80$

2) $7n = 91$

3) $.5n = 100$

4) $19n = 323$

5) $\frac{1}{4}n = 25$

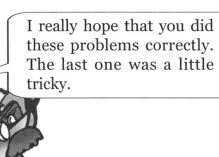

I really hope that you did these problems correctly. The last one was a little tricky.

1) $2n = 80$

$\frac{2n}{2} = \frac{80}{2}$ $n = 40$

2) $7n = 91$

$\frac{7n}{7} = \frac{91}{7}$ $n = 13$

3) $.5n = 100$

$\frac{.5n}{.5} = \frac{100}{.5}$ $n = 200$

4) $19n = 323$

$\frac{19n}{19} = \frac{323}{19}$ $n = 17$

5) $\frac{1}{4}n = 25$

$\frac{1}{4}n \times 4 = 25 \times 4$

$n = 100$

There is a kind of equation that is a little tricky when you try to have only one n. This is an equation such as the one that I've written on the blackboard.

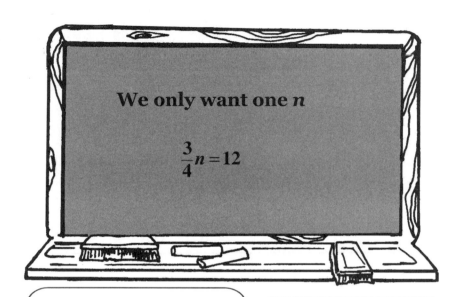

We only want one n

$$\frac{3}{4}n = 12$$

I know how to turn the $\frac{3}{4}n$ into only one n. You simply multiply by the reciprocal of $\frac{3}{4}$, which is $\frac{4}{3}$.

What in the world is a reciprocal? I am very confused!

Every fraction has a special fraction friend called a reciprocal that can turn the fraction into one. Look at how I multiplied $\frac{3}{4}$ by $\frac{4}{3}$ to turn $\frac{3}{4}$ into one. Of course I multiplied the other side of the equation by $\frac{4}{3}$.

We only want one n

$$\frac{3}{4}n = 12 \qquad \frac{4}{3} \times \frac{3}{4}n = 12 \times \frac{4}{3}$$

I know how to find reciprocals! All you do is turn the fraction upside down. The reciprocal of $\frac{5}{6}$ would be $\frac{6}{5}$. This is much easier than I thought.

The equation is very easy to solve now. $n = 16$

$$1n = 12 \times \frac{4}{3} \quad n = 16$$

Try these equations. Remember that you can turn a number into 1 by multiplying by its reciprocal.

1) $\dfrac{5}{8}n = 40$

2) $\dfrac{2}{7}n = 26$

3) $\dfrac{1}{11}n = 9$

4) $\dfrac{7}{8}n = 126$

5) $\dfrac{3}{5}n = 4.35$

Here are the answers. I hope you didn't get as stressed out as I did when I did the problems.

1) $\dfrac{8}{5}x\dfrac{5}{8}n = 40\,x\,\dfrac{8}{5}$ n=64

2) $\dfrac{7}{2}x\dfrac{2}{7}n = 26\,x\,\dfrac{7}{2}$ n=91

3) $\dfrac{11}{1}x\dfrac{1}{11}n = 9\,x\,\dfrac{11}{1}$ n=99

4) $\dfrac{8}{7}x\dfrac{7}{8}n = 126\,x\,\dfrac{8}{7}$ n=144

5) $\dfrac{5}{3}x\dfrac{3}{5}n = 4.35\,x\,\dfrac{5}{3}$ n=7.25

Level 1

1) $2n + 8 = 24$

2) $5n - 5 = 85$

3) $2n + 8 - n = 20$

4) $7n + 4 + n - 5 = 63$

5) $2n + 1 = n + 10$

6) $2n - 7 = 0$

7) $n + 2n + 3n + 4n = 2 + 3 + 4 + 5 + 6$

8) $\frac{1}{2}n + 1\frac{1}{2}n = -10$

9) $4n - 8 = n + 1$

10) $100n = 100$

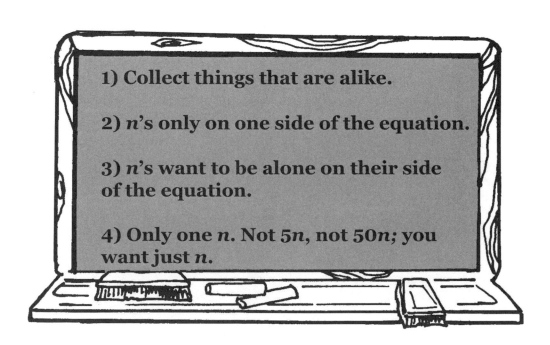

1) Collect things that are alike.

2) *n*'s only on one side of the equation.

3) *n*'s want to be alone on their side of the equation.

4) Only one *n*. Not 5*n*, not 50*n*; you want just *n*.

Level 2

1) $n - n = 10 - n$

2) $2n - 1\frac{1}{2}n = 59$

3) $2n + 10 = 3n + 5$

4) $2n = 4n$

5) $n + 9n - 8 - 5 = 2n + 3$

6) $\frac{1}{10}n = 100$

7) $n^2 = 64$

8) $n + 9n - 90 = 0$

9) $n^2 + 9 = 34$

10) $10n - 9n + 8n - 7n + 6n = 10 - 9 + 8 - 7 + 6$

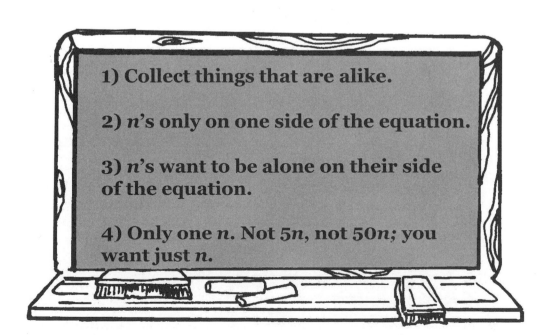

1) Collect things that are alike.

2) n's only on one side of the equation.

3) n's want to be alone on their side of the equation.

4) Only one n. Not 5n, not 50n; you want just n.

Level 3

1) $-n = -50$

2) $-\dfrac{1}{8}n = 80$

3) $n^2 = \dfrac{1}{4}$

4) $n = 3n - \dfrac{1}{2}$

5) $10n = .5$

6) $-5n - 5n - 5 = 5$

7) $\dfrac{1}{11}n = 11$

8) $\dfrac{3}{5}n = 1$

9) $1 - n = n - 1$

10) $n^2 = 6\dfrac{1}{4}$

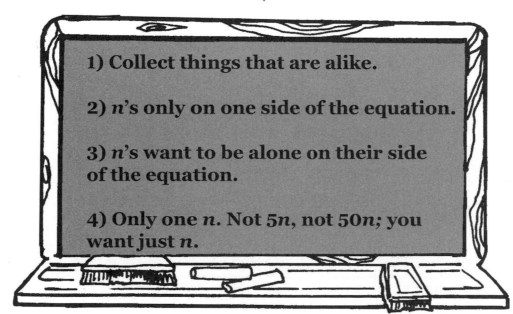

1) **Collect things that are alike.**

2) **n's only on one side of the equation.**

3) **n's want to be alone on their side of the equation.**

4) **Only one n. Not $5n$, not $50n$; you want just n.**

Einstein Level

1) $n^2 - 1 = \dfrac{-99}{100}$

2) $-n = n$

3) $n + .07n = \$90.95$

4) $\dfrac{1}{n^2} = \dfrac{3}{192}$

5) $n + \dfrac{1}{2}n + \dfrac{1}{4}n + \dfrac{1}{8}n + \dfrac{1}{16}n = 19{,}375$

6) $\dfrac{1}{n} + \dfrac{2}{n} + \dfrac{3}{n} = 1$

7) $5^{n-1} - 15{,}625$

8) $2^n = 4^{n-3}$

9) $\dfrac{1}{n} + \dfrac{2}{n} + \dfrac{3}{n} + \dfrac{4}{n} = 1$

10) $\dfrac{1}{n} + \dfrac{3}{5} = 1$

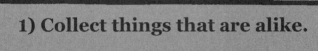

1) Collect things that are alike.

2) n's only on one side of the equation.

3) n's want to be alone on their side of the equation.

4) Only one n. Not $5n$, not $50n$; you want just n.

Super Einstein

Solve for n: $\dfrac{31}{170} = \dfrac{1}{5\dfrac{1}{2\dfrac{1}{n}}}$

Solving Algebra Problems

A sandwich and a drink together cost $10. If the sandwich cost $9 more than the drink, how much does the drink cost?

A sandwich and a drink together cost $10. If the sandwich cost $9 more than the drink, how much does the drink cost?

I don't need algebra to solve that! The answer is very obvious...the drink cost $1.

Well, actually that is wrong. Watch how algebra corrects your flawed thinking.

Language of Algebra
Drink: n
Sandwich: $n + 9$

Equation:
Drink + Sandwich = $10
$n + (n+9) = \$10$
$2n + 9 = 10$
$2n = 1$
$n = .5$ dollars or 50 cents

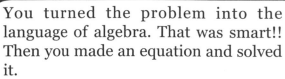

You turned the problem into the language of algebra. That was smart!! Then you made an equation and solved it.

Language of Algebra
Drink: n
Sandwich: $n + 9$

Equation:
Drink + Sandwich = \$10
$n + (n+9) = \$10$
$2n + 9 = 10$
$2n = 1$
$n = .5$ dollars or 50 cents

Okay, I see that you subtracted 9 from both sides. Now both sides are divided by 2 and it turns out that $n = 50$ cents

Wow! Algebra is sure a great way to correct flawed thinking!

I would like you to meet my neighbor. His name is Mr. Yoda and he wants you to guess his age.

He has written a hint on the blackboard to help you with your guesses.

I am 20 times older than your teacher, who is 22 years older than his son Dan. The total of our ages is 902 years. How old am I?

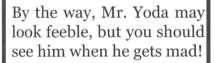

By the way, Mr. Yoda may look feeble, but you should see him when he gets mad!

Let's first change everyone's age into the language of algebra.

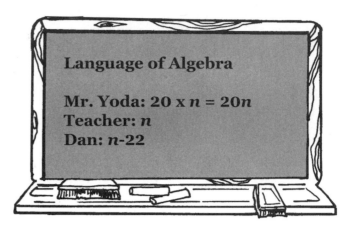

Language of Algebra

Mr. Yoda: 20 x *n* = 20*n*
Teacher: *n*
Dan: *n*-22

Dan's age is ***n*-22** because he is 22 years younger than the teacher.

Why did you call the teacher's age *n*? Could you have called Mr. Yoda's age *n*?

We can call anybody ***n***, but look how messy it is if we call Mr. Yoda ***n***.

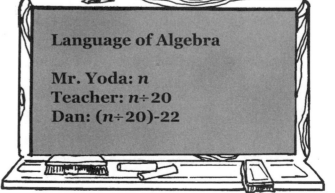

Language of Algebra

Mr. Yoda: *n*
Teacher: *n*÷20
Dan: (*n*÷20)-22

That is messy! Let's go back to calling the teacher's age *n*.

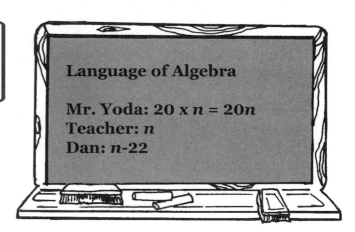

Language of Algebra

Mr. Yoda: $20 \times n = 20n$
Teacher: n
Dan: $n\text{-}22$

Now let's add all their ages. Because we know that the ages add up to 902 years, we can write an equation.

Add ages: $20n + n + n - 22$

Collect: $22n - 22$

Equation: $22n - 22 = 902$

Add 22 to each side: $22n = 924$

Divide both sides by 22: $n = 42$

If *n* is equal to 42, then Yoda's age is $42 \times 20 = 840$. The reason we multiplied by 20 is because Yoda's age is $20n$.

Algebra sure made that problem very easy!

Level 1

1) Laura weighs 45 pounds more than her pet dog. When they are on the scale together, they weigh 85 pounds. How much does Laura weigh?

Language of algebra:
Dog: n
Laura:
Equation:

2) Stanley bought a ruler and a yardstick for $1.25. If the yardstick cost 45 cents more than the ruler, what was the cost of the yardstick?

Language of algebra:
Ruler: n
Yardstick:
Equation:

3) Jane is twice as old as Joel. If their ages total 63 years, how old is Joel?

Language of algebra:
Joel: n
Jane:
Equation:

4) The price of a cheap backpack is $15 less than an expensive backpack. When Emily bought both, she paid $75. What is the cost of the cheap backpack?

Language of algebra:
Cheap backpack: n
Expensive backpack:
Equation:

5) If two consecutive even numbers are added, the sum is equal to 226. What is the smaller of the two numbers?

Language of algebra:
Smaller number: n
Larger number:
Equation:

Level 2

1) Mathew's cat weighs 10 pounds more than his pet hamster. His dog weighs the same as his cat. If the weight of all three pets is 35 pounds, how much does his hamster weigh?

Language of algebra:
Hamster: n
Cat:
Dog:
Equation:

2) Wendy is paid $7.50 per hour plus a bonus of $80 each week. Last week Wendy earned $312.50. How many hours did Wendy work last week?

Language of algebra:
Hours worked: n
Hourly pay:
Bonus:
Equation:

3) Dennis was getting in shape for a marathon. The first day of the week he ran n miles. Dennis then added a mile to his run each day. By the end of the week (7 days), he had run a total of 70 miles. How many miles did Dennis run the first day?

Language of algebra:
1st day: n
2nd day:
3rd day:
4th day:
5th day:
6th day:
7th day:
Equation:

4) Luke and Dan's total debt is $72. If Luke's debt is three times Dan's debt, what is Dan's debt?

Language of algebra:
Dan's debt: n
Luke's debt:
Equation:

I have three times the debt that you have. Are you jealous?

I hate to tell you this, but debt is a bad thing, not a good thing!

I think I am in a little trouble. No one told me that debt is a bad thing!

5) Jason has an equal number of nickels and dimes. The total value of his nickels and dimes is $2.25. How many nickels does Jason have?

Language of algebra:
Number of nickels: n
Number of dimes: n
Value of the nickels:
Value of the dimes:
Equation:

Level 3

1) Adam took money from his savings account to use as spending money on a trip to San Antonio. On Monday he spent half his money. On Tuesday he spent half of what was left. On Wednesday he again spent half of his remaining money. On Thursday he woke up with very little money left, but again spent half of it. If Adam started the vacation with n dollars, how much money did he have at the end of the day on Thursday?

Language of algebra:
Monday:
Tuesday:
Wednesday:
Thursday:

2) Sonia visited a park in California that had redwood trees. When Sonia asked how tall a certain large redwood tree was, the ranger said that he wouldn't tell its height, but would give Sonia a clue. How tall is the redwood tree Sonia asked about?

Language of algebra:
Ranger's height: n
Tree's height:
Smaller tree's height:
Equation:

The tree is 64 times my height. The tree is also 112 feet taller than the tree next to it. The two trees plus my height total 597.5 feet.

3) A trapezoid has one base that is 120% of the length of the other base. The two sides are each 1/2 the length of the smaller base. If the perimeter of the trapezoid is 54.4 inches, what is the length of the smaller base of the trapezoid?

n

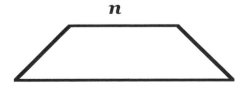

4) The sales tax on a computer was $33.60. If the sales tax rate is 7%, how much did the computer cost without tax?

Language of algebra:
Computer: n
Tax:
Equation:

5) A barn contains cows, ducks, and a 3-legged dog named Tripod. There are twice as many cows as ducks in the barn and a total of 313 legs. How many ducks are there in the barn?

Language of algebra:
Number of ducks: n
Number of cows:
Duck legs:
Cow legs:
Tripod's legs:
Equation:

Einstein Level

1) In the year 1980, Ric was twice as old as Nancy who was twice as old as Michael. In the year 1992 Ric, Nancy, and Michael's ages added up to 78 years. How old was Ric in 1980?

2) Erin has 72 stamps in her stamp drawer along with a quarter, two dimes and seven pennies. She has 3 times as many 3-cent stamps as 37-cent stamps and half the number of 5-cent stamps as 37-cent stamps. The value of the stamps and coins is $8.28. How many 37-cent stamps does Erin have?

3) When each side of a square is doubled in length, its area increases by 432 square inches. What is the size of the original square?

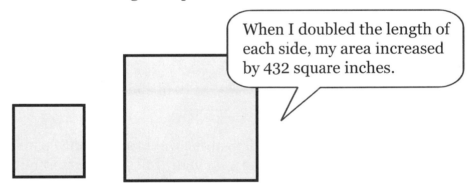

When I doubled the length of each side, my area increased by 432 square inches.

4) The phone company charges Rachel 12 cents per minute for her long distance calls. A discount company called Rachel and offered her long distance service for 1/2 cent per minute, but will charge a $46 monthly fee. How many minutes per month must Rachel talk on the phone to make the discount a better deal?

5) A suitcase contains nickels, dimes and quarters. There are $2\frac{1}{2}$ times as many dimes as nickels and 5 times the number of quarters as the number of nickels. If the coins have a value of $24.80, how many nickels are there in the suitcase?

Super Einstein

Laura found a roll of fencing in her garage.
She couldn't decide whether to fence in a
square garden or a round garden with the fencing.

Laura did some calculations and found that a circular garden would give her 1380 more square
feet than a square garden. How many feet of fencing were in the roll that Laura found? (Round
to the nearest foot.)

Logic

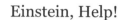

So now we know that all cats are animals, so all animals must be cats!

Einstein, Help!

What you have just experienced is an example of poor logic.

Because all cats are animals doesn't mean the reverse of it is true!

Look at some other examples...

1) **All children are people, but not all people are children.**

2) **All dogs are mammals, but all mammals are not dogs.**

3) **All rectangles are quadrilaterals, but not all quadrilaterals are rectangles.**

4) **All rectangles are parallelograms, but all parallelograms are not rectangles.**

5) **All squares are rectangles, but not all rectangles are squares.**

Here's a logic problem that is a little more difficult:

Whenever Lauren is in math class, she has her calculator. Lauren has her calculator, so we know she must be in math class. Is this true?

It is not true! Even though Lauren is never in math class without her calculator, she might have her calculator in her pocket during history, or even during lunch hour.

Level 1

1) If all A's are B's, then all B's are A's. Is this true?

2) If Susan is riding her bike, she always wears her helmet. Susan is wearing her helmet. Do we know that Susan is riding her bike?

3) All squares are rectangles and all rectangles are parallelograms, therefore all squares are parallelograms. Is this true?

4) Dale has a box that contains 20 American quarters and 20 Canadian quarters. If he takes them from the box one at a time, how many must he remove before he is guaranteed to have 5 quarters from the same country?

5) Which drawing best describes the fact that all squares are rectangles, but not all rectangles are squares?

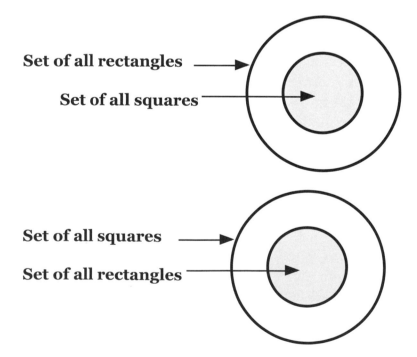

Set of all rectangles

Set of all squares

Set of all squares

Set of all rectangles

Level 2

1) If Dan does not study, he will fail his History test. Dan failed his History test. Do we know that he did not study?

2) If it is raining, I will get wet if I go outside. I went outside and got wet. Do I know it was raining when I went outside?

3) Which drawing best describes the situation in the previous problem?

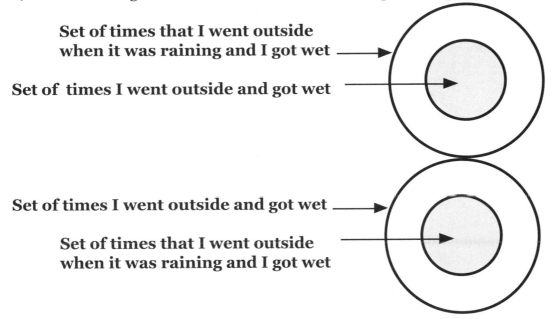

Set of times that I went outside when it was raining and I got wet

Set of times I went outside and got wet

Set of times I went outside and got wet

Set of times that I went outside when it was raining and I got wet

4) Corvettes are known as sporty cars that can travel at high rates of speed. It is therefore assumed that they are much more dangerous than minivans. An owner of a Corvette points out that when statistics are studied, there are far more deaths each year from crashes that involve minivans than crashes that involve Corvettes, so Corvettes must be safer than minivans. The statistics the Corvette owner sites are correct. Is his logic faulty? Why or why not?

5) Bashar just read that many more car accidents occur within 30 miles of one's home. He decided that he would wear his seat belt only when he is driving within 30 miles from his home and not on long trips because it is obviously safer to travel when you are more than 30 miles from your home.

Explain why Bashar's logic is flawed.

Level 3

1) A cup that is filled with equal parts red, green, and blue dye spills half of its contents. Enough green dye is then poured into the cup to fill it again. What is the ratio of red to green to blue dye now?

2) If all four sides of a rectangle are equal, then the rectangle is a square. If a figure is a square, then its diagonals cut each of the corner angles into two equal angles. Figure A is a four-sided figure whose diagonals cut each of the corner angles into two equal angles. Can we say that the figure must be a square? Why or why not?

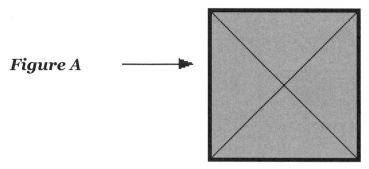

Figure A

3) All of the players on a soccer team who picked goalie as their favorite position are left-handed. Saul is on the soccer team and is left-handed. Does this mean that goalie is Saul's favorite position? A set picture that shows this situation is shown below.

Place the following four categories with the correct part of the set diagram:

a) All players on the soccer team
b) Players who picked goalie as their favorite position
c) Right-handed players
d) Left-handed players

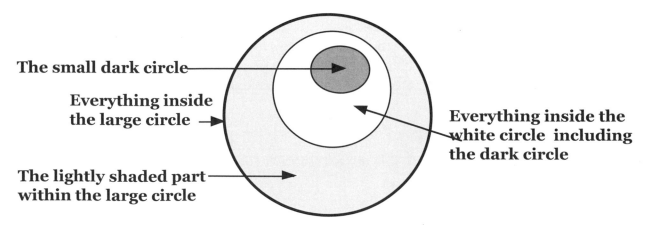

4) Before you is a 3-quart container, a 5-quart container and a sink full of water. There are no markings on either container to show how many quarts are in each one. All you know is that when the 3-quart container is full, it contains three quarts. You also know that when the 5-quart container is full, it contains five quarts. Your task is to place exactly four quarts in the 5-quart container. How would you accomplish this task?

5) If Tanya eats the box of donuts before she goes to bed, she'll wake up in a fog the next day. If she is in a fog, she will not do well on the SAT test that she will take the next day. If she doesn't do well on that SAT test, she will not get a scholarship to college and will have to pay her own way. Can we conclude that if Tanya eats the box of donuts before she goes to bed that she will not get a scholarship to college?

Einstein Level

1) A family is taking a cross-country trip of 3000 miles by car. They are bringing two spare tires with them and want all six tires to go an equal distance. How many miles will each tire go?

2) If the raccoon is innocent, then the opossum is not lying.
If the rabbit is being truthful, then the opossum is lying.
If the rabbit is lying, then it has something to gain from lying.

The owl just found out that the rabbit would gain nothing from lying. Is the raccoon guilty or innocent? Why?

3) There are two containers. One holds exactly 7 quarts and the other holds exactly 9 quarts. There are no markings on the containers that allow you to know when they contain one, two, three, four, five, six or eight quarts.

You have a tub full of water and you can fill and empty the 7 and 9 quart container however you wish. How can you end up with exactly 8 quarts in the 9 quart container?

4) Use the information below to determine the weight of 500 gallons of water.

   a) There are 1.057 quarts in a liter and 4 quarts in a gallon.
   b) A cubic decimeter of water is a liter of water.
   c) A cubic decimeter of water weighs one kilogram.
   d) There are 2.2 pounds in a kilogram.

5) After a long journey, you finally arrive at the edge of a deep gorge where there are two identical bridges from which to choose your path to the other side.

One bridge is safe, while the other is very dangerous and has caused the deaths of hundreds of travelers. The owner of the first bridge is a talking rat, while the owner of the second bridge is a talking frog. Friends told you before you left that one of the bridge owners always tells the truth, while the other always lies.

You are allowed one question to ask of either the frog or the rat to find out which bridge is the safe bridge. What is the question that you would ask?

Super Einstein

Three people went to lunch and bought a large meal which they all split. The total cost, including tip, was $30. Each person paid $10 to the waitress and started to leave the restaurant. As they left, the waitress came running up to them with five dollars saying that she made a mistake and that the meal and tip should have cost only $25.

The waitress then gave each person one dollar, but didn't know how to split the remaining two dollars. They told her to keep the extra two dollars as an additional tip.

When the people started talking about what had just happened, they started getting confused. They had each paid $10 for the meal and received one dollar back, so they each really paid $9 for the meal for a total of $27. Add the two dollars of extra tip and the total is $29. Where did the extra one dollar go?

Power of Ratios

I just heard that a person who is worth one billion dollars gave one million dollars to a charity. I wish I was that generous! I only gave $10 to charity last year.

Don't feel bad. You are actually more generous than the billionaire.

?

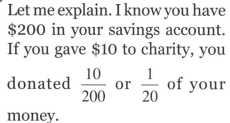

Let me explain. I know you have $200 in your savings account. If you gave $10 to charity, you donated $\frac{10}{200}$ or $\frac{1}{20}$ of your money.

Look at the billionaire's donation compared to how much money he has...

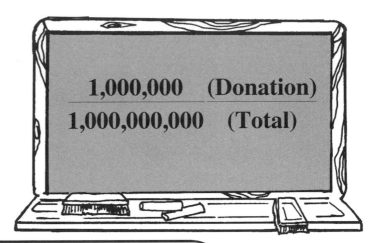

$$\frac{1{,}000{,}000 \quad \text{(Donation)}}{1{,}000{,}000{,}000 \quad \text{(Total)}}$$

When you reduce the fraction, you find that the billionaire donated $\frac{1}{1000}$ of his money, while you donated $\frac{1}{20}$ of your money.

I guess I am more generous than the billionaire!

I've heard that some ants that weigh $\frac{1}{10}$ of an ounce can lift things that weigh 5 ounces.

If a 150 pound person could lift "proportionally" as much as an ant, would he be able to lift a 4,000 pound car?

We can solve this problem by putting the two ratios next to each other.

$$\frac{\frac{1}{10} \text{ ounce (weight of ant)}}{5 \text{ ounces (amount ant can lift)}} = \frac{150 \text{ pounds (weight of person)}}{n \text{ (amount person can lift)}}$$

$$\frac{\frac{1}{10} \text{ ounce (weight of ant)}}{5 \text{ ounces (amount ant can lift)}} = \frac{150 \text{ pounds (weight of person)}}{n \text{ (amount person can lift)}}$$

Now cross-multiply to solve the problem.

Cross-multiply: $\dfrac{1}{10}n = 750$ or $.1n = 750$

Divide by .1: $\dfrac{.1n}{.1} = \dfrac{750}{.1}$ $n = 7500$

If a 150 pound person was "proportionally" as strong as an ant, he could lift 7,500 pounds! That's almost two 4,000 pound cars!

Level 1

1) The scale on a map is 1 inch = 60 miles. If two cities are 75 miles apart, how far apart are they on the map?

2) A school has a boy to girl ratio of 6:7. If there are 288 boys, how many girls are there?

3) Erica is 5 feet tall and has a shadow of 2 feet. A nearby tree has a shadow of 18 feet. How tall is the tree?

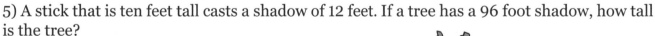

4) If there are 9000 seconds in 2.5 hours, how many hours are there in 13,500 seconds?

5) A stick that is ten feet tall casts a shadow of 12 feet. If a tree has a 96 foot shadow, how tall is the tree?

Level 2

1) A person who had $1,000,000 gave $100 to charity. How much must a student who has $100 give to charity to give proportionally the same as the millionaire?

2) A 1.5 inch tall preying mantis will sometimes hold its ground and attempt to fight a person who is 6 feet tall. If a person who is 6 feet tall engaged in a battle with an animal that was proportionally as tall as the person is to the preying mantis, how tall would the animal be?

3) A recipe that makes 25 oatmeal cookies calls for 2.5 cups of oats and one cup of sugar. Jerry needs to make 195 cookies for his school party. How many cups of oats will he need?

4) A flea is very small, but can jump very high. For example, a flea that is 1/8 inch tall can jump 12 inches in height. If a child who is 4 feet tall had the ability to jump like a flea, how high could she jump?

5) If 3.75 inches on a map are equal to 18.75 miles, how many miles are 5 inches equal to?

Level 3

1) A giant tortoise can live 175 years in captivity. The gastrotrich, which is a small aquatic animal, has a life-span of only 3 days (72 hours). If a gastrotrich died after 36 hours, a giant tortoise that lived 87.5 years would live proportionally the same because they both would have died halfway through their life-span.

How long would a giant tortoise live if it lived proportionally the same as a gastrotrich that died after 50 hours?

2) A goal for many elite runners is to complete a mile in 4 minutes. At what speed (in miles per hour) is a runner traveling when he completes a mile in 4 minutes?

3) A yardstick casts a shadow of 8 inches. At the same time, a tree casts a shadow of 52 feet. How tall is the tree?

4) Ric sold a total of 75 books during the first 22 days of May. If he continues to sell books at the same rate, how many books will he sell in the month of May?

5) A typical human adult weighs 150 pounds, while a human newborn weighs approximately 7 pounds. An adult female Western Grey Kangaroo weighs about 30 kilograms and gives birth to babies who are approximately one gram. If human babies were proportionally the same weight to adults as Western Grey Kangaroos babies, how much would a human newborn weigh?

Did you know that there are 1000 grams in one kilogram?

Warning: There is a number in this problem that you do not need for the ratio. This confuses a lot of students, so be careful.

Einstein Level

1) What is the ratio of the area of a circle to the area of a square drawn around that circle? Express your answer in terms of π.

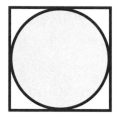

2) In the year 1999, Hicham El Guerrouj of Morocco set a new world record when he ran a mile in 3 minutes 43.13 seconds. What was his speed in miles per hour? (Round your answer to the nearest hundredth.)

3) If a Canadian dollar is worth $.82 in American money, how much is an American dollar worth in Canadian money?

4) If a speedometer indicates that a car is traveling at 65 kilometers per hour, how fast is the car traveling in miles per hour? (Round to the nearest tenth.)

Did you know that a kilometer is equal to .621 miles?

5) A broken clock that loses 12 minutes every hour is set at 12:00 noon at the same time a normal clock has its time set to 12:00 noon. When the broken clock reaches 12:00 midnight, what will the normal clock read?

Super Einstein

The world record for the mile in the year 1865 was held by Richard Webster of England when he completed a mile in 4 minutes and 36.5 seconds. The world record in 1999 was set by Hicham El Guerrrouj when he ran a mile in 3 minutes and 43.13 seconds.

If both men ran the mile together, how many feet behind would Richard Webster be when Hichem El Guerrouj crossed the finish line?

Good luck trying to catch me. I have the shoes, the water and the attitude!

Function Machines

7, 12, 17, 22, ?

The next number in this sequence is easy to find------ it is 27. What is the 1000th number in this sequence?

The 1000th number is easy to find. All you do is add 5 each time. Give me a couple hours and I will use my calculator to find the answer!

I don't know about you, but I have better things to do than add 5 on a calculator for two hours. I hope there is an easier way to find the answer!

Actually there is a machine that will find the answer for you in about 10 seconds. It is called a function machine.

First look at this simple function machine. When you put a 1 in (the 1 stands for the first number) a 6 comes out. When you put a 2 in (the 2 stands for the second number) a 12 comes out.

I know what the machine is doing. I will open the door and see if I am correct. The machine is multiplying by 6. I was right!

I like how you put an **n** through the machine. If the machine multiplies by 6, then **6n** will come out.

Let's get back to our original problem. I am going to put 1,2,3, and 4 under each of the numbers because they are the 1st, 2nd, 3rd and 4th numbers. I will also put a 1000 for the 1000th number.

7,	12,	17,	22,		?
1	2	3	4		1000

You will appear smarter if you call the 1st number the first term. I am going to refer to the numbers as the 1st term, the 2nd term, the 3rd term and the 4th term. I will even call the number that we are looking for the 1000th term!

7	12	17	22	?
1st term	2nd term	3rd term	4th term	1000th term

7	12	17	22	?
1st term	2nd term	3rd term	4th term	1000th term

7	12	17	22	?
1st term	2nd term	3rd term	4th term	1000th term

That makes sense. I am going to make sure the function machine works. If I send a 2 through the machine, a 12 should come out.

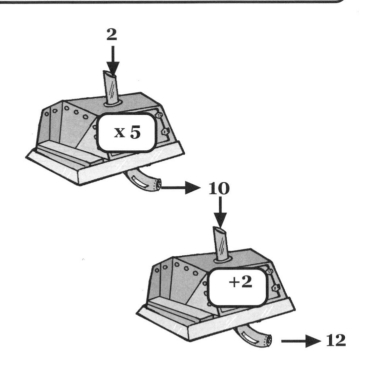

Now I am ready to put 1000 into the machine. When I do send the 1000 through the function machine, 5002 comes out. That was sure easier than using a calculator for 2 hours.

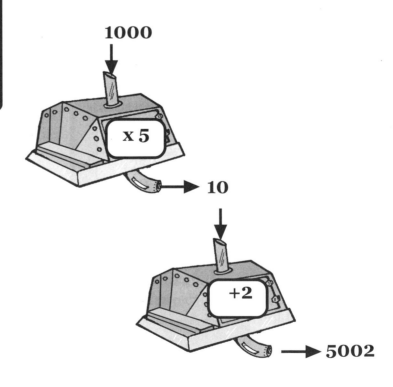

Try these problems. Remember that if the amount each number grows by is 4, then the first function machine is multiply by 4. If the amount each number grows by is 7, then the first function machine is multiply by 7.

1) Find the 500th term.

8, 12, 16, 20,   ?
1   2   3   4   500

2) Find the 1000th term.

1, 9, 17, 25,   ?
1   2   3   4   1000

Problems 4 and 5 are a little tricky because they are not going up by a certain number. Because they are going down, the function machine is a little bit strange.

3) Find the 5000th term.

3, 10, 17, 24,   ?
1   2   3   4   5000

4) Find the 100th term.

10, 5, 0, -5,   ?
1   2   3   4   100

5) Find the 500th term.

100, 80, 60, 40,   ?
1   2   3   4   500

Answers

Let's see how you did. I hope you figured out that the first function machine in problems #4 and #5 multiplied by a negative number.

1) Find the 500th term.

8, 12, 16, 20,	?
1 2 3 4	500

Function machine is x4 plus 4
500th term is 2004

2) Find the 1000th term.

1, 9, 17, 25,	?
1 2 3 4	1000

Function machine is x8 minus 7
1000th term is 7993

3) Find the 5000th term.

3, 10, 17, 24,	?
1 2 3 4	5000

Function machine is x7 minus 4
5000th term is 34,996

4) Find the 100th term.

10, 5, 0, -5,	?
1 2 3 4	100

Function machine is x-5 plus 15
100th term is -485

5) Find the 500th term.

100, 80, 60, 40,	?
1 2 3 4	500

Function machine is x-20 plus 120
500th term is -9880

Now that you are getting pretty good at these, I am going to give you a problem that looks confusing. In this problem you will need to go through the function machine in reverse.

4, 7, 10, 13,   **256**
1   2   3   4   ?

1

x 3

3

+1

4

The problem is asking you to find out what term the number 256 is in the sequence. The first thing we need to do is find the function machine. Because there is a difference of 3, the function machine is x3 then plus 1.

Now we have to send the number through the function machine in reverse. When we do this we must change the operations to the opposite operation. Plus will become minus and multiply will become divide.

256 minus 1 = 255. Now we will divide by 3. The number 256 is the 85th term in this sequence.

85

÷3

255

-1

256

Let's try one more. For this problem, we need to find out the term for the number 234. It is pretty easy to see that the function machine is **x 2.5 plus 1.5.** (1 x 2.5 plus 1.5 is equal to 4 and 2 x 2.5 plus 1.5 is equal to 6.5) Now go through the function machine in reverse.

4, 6.5, 9, 11.5,   **234**

1   2   3   4   ?

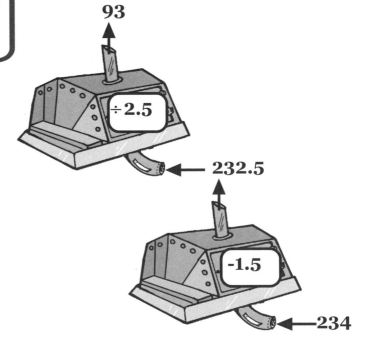

93

÷2.5

232.5

-1.5

234

Try these problems. Remember that if the amount each number grows is 4, then the first function machine is multiply by 4. If the amount each number grows is 7, then the first function machine is multiply by 7.

1) What term is the number 1222?

12, 23, 34 , 45,	1222
1 2 3 4	?

2) What term is the number -223?

1, -6, -13, -20,	-223
1 2 3 4	?

Problems 4 and 5 have a new kind of function machine they do. Very carefully think and solve it you will. A clue I will give you----exponents. Good luck!!

3) What term is the number 388?

3, 10, 17, 24,	388
1 2 3 4	?

4) What term is the number 6561?

1, 4, 9, 16,	6561
1 2 3 4	?

5) What term is the number 3375?

1, 8, 27, 64,	3375
1 2 3 4	?

Answers

I hope you remembered to change to the opposite operations when you went through the function machines in reverse.

1) What term is the number 1222?

12, 23, 34 , 45,	1222
1 2 3 4	?

Function machine: 11 x n + 1
Reverse: (1222 - 1) ÷ 11 = 111

2) What term is the number -223?

1, -6, -13, -20,	-223
1 2 3 4	?

Function machine: -7 x n + 8
Reverse: (-223 - 8) ÷ -7 = 33

3) What term is the number 388?

3, 10, 17, 24,	388
1 2 3 4	?

Function machine: 7 x n - 4
Reverse: (388 + 4) ÷ 7 = 56

4) What term is the number 6561?

1, 4, 9, 16,	6561
1 2 3 4	?

Function machine: n x n
Reverse: Square root of 6561 = 81

5) What term is the number 3375?

1, 8, 27, 64,	3375
1 2 3 4	?

Function machine: n x n x n
Reverse: Cube root of 3375----or
                    n x n x n = 3375 n=15

Level 1

1) 5,10,15,20
What is the next number?
What is the 100th term?

When you put a 1 (1st term) into the
machine, you want a 5 to come out.

When you put a 2 (2nd term) into the
machine, you want a 10 to come out.

What is the machine doing to the numbers you put in?

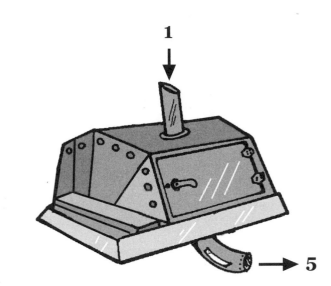

2) 8,11,14,17,20

What is the next number?
What is the 150th term?
Hint: You will need two machines.

3) 0,7,14,21

What is the next number?
What is the 1000th term?
Hint: You will need two machines.

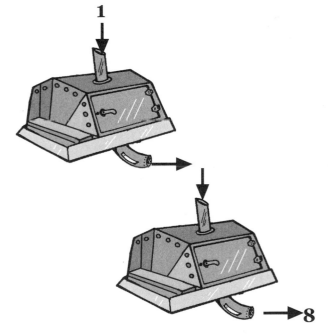

4) 1, 1/2, 1/3, 1/4, 1/5

What is the next number?
What is the 89th term of the sequence?

5) 2,   4,   6,   8.............................1000
 1st 2nd 3rd 4th   ?

The next number is obviously 10. What term is the number 1000?
Hint: Go through the function machine backwards.

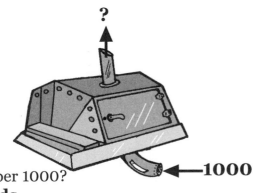

Level 2

1) 1.25, 2, 2.75, 3.5
What is the 100th term?

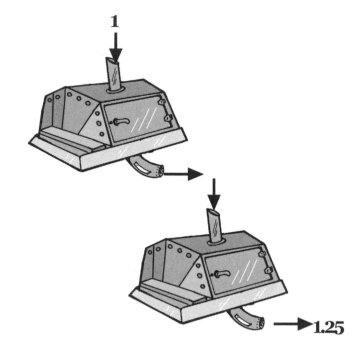

2) 3, 8, 13, 18...........................5008
What term is the number 5008?

3) -11, -9, -7, -5, -3
What is the next number?
What is the 200th term in the sequence?

4) 100, 75, 50, 25, 0, -25
What is the next number?
What is the 100th term?

5) 5, 14, 23, 32, 41......................1895
What term is the number 1895?

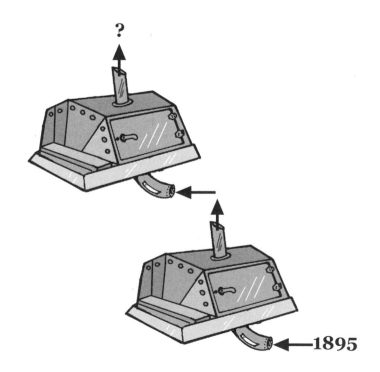

Level 3

1) 1, 4, 9, 16, 25
What is the next number?
What is the 50th term?

I have a hint for you. The function machines do not always have to be multiplying, dividing, adding, or subtracting. They can do things that exponents do to numbers.

2) 7, 10, 15, 22
What is the next number in the sequence?
What is the 500th term?

3) 1, 8, 27, 64
What is the 10th term?

4) 10,   1000,   100,000,   10,000,000
What power of 10 is the 80th term?

5) 1/2, 3, 51/2, 8...................203
What term is the number 203?

Einstein Level

1) 1, 1/2, 1/4, 1/8, 1/16
The next number in the sequence is 1/32.
What is the function machine you would use
to find the nth term of this sequence?

Hint: Look at the denominators.

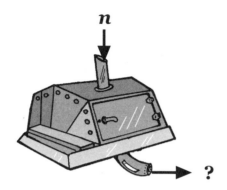

2) Mike received a penny on December 1st. On December 2nd he received 2 cents, December
3rd another 4 cents and December 4th he received 8 cents. If his money continues to
double, how much will he earn on December 25th?

3) 3, 6, 12, 24, 48
What is the function machine for this sequence?

4) 9, 3, 1, 1/3, 1/9
What is the next number in this sequence?
What is the function machine for this sequence?

5) How many squares of any size are in this figure?
(Assume all are squares)

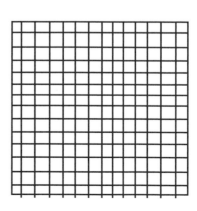

Super Einstein

There is a tower with 64 rings like the one shown below. The one below has only 8 rings, but your tower has 64 rings. Your task is to move the 64 rings to the far left post, but you must follow some rules:

1) **Move only one ring at a time.**
2) **Rings can only be placed on a post. (Not held or placed on the table.)**
3) **A larger ring can never be placed on a smaller ring.**
4) **You will be given a dollar for each move you take.**
5) **You must take as few moves as possible to accomplish the task or you will receive no money.**

How much money will you receive? (You can express your answer in exponent form)

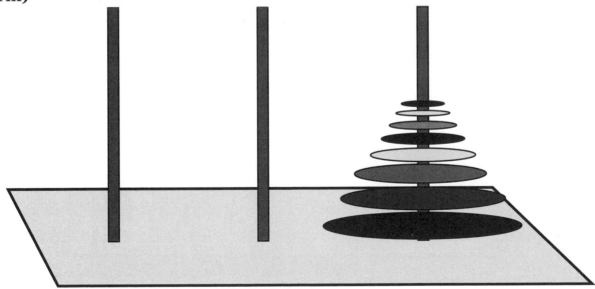

Don't be Fooled

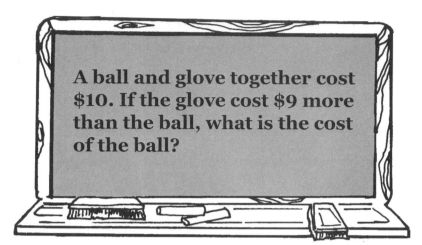

I have an easy problem for you. Believe it or not, a lot of people miss this problem so be careful!

A ball and glove together cost $10. If the glove cost $9 more than the ball, what is the cost of the ball?

That problem is so easy Einstein. I am insulted that you would think I would find it difficult. The answer is obviously $1!

Sorry, you **were** fooled. The answer is not $1.

If you think about the problem, you can see that if the ball cost $1, then the glove must cost $1 + $9 = $10 (the glove is $9 more than the ball.)

The problem said that the ball and glove together cost $10. $1 + $10 = $11 so something is wrong with your answer of $1.

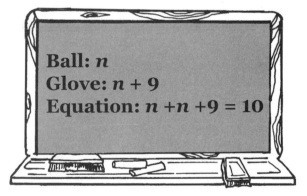

Ball: $1
Glove: $10
Total: $1 + $10 = $11

Let's use algebra to help our brain think a little better.

Ball: n
Glove: $n + 9$
Equation: $n + n + 9 = 10$

I see! You call the ball n, so the glove must be $n + 9$ because it cost $9 more than the ball.

The equation is $n + n + 9 = 10$ because when you add the ball and the glove it adds up to $10.

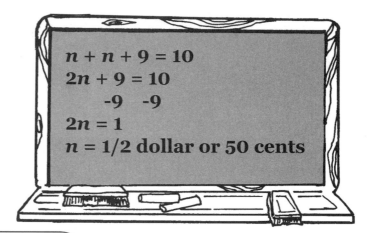

$$n + n + 9 = 10$$
$$2n + 9 = 10$$
$$-9-9$$
$$2n = 1$$
$$n = 1/2 \text{ dollar or 50 cents}$$

Now simply solve the equation. The ball cost 50 cents.

The story I am about to tell you is about what can happen when a mind is fooled by a problem. In this true story, 114 people died and over 200 were injured.

The Kansas City Hyatt Regency Hotel Disaster

On July 17, 1981, 2000 people gathered in the lobby of the Kansas City Hyatt Regency Hotel to either watch or take part in a popular dance contest. In addition to those in the lobby, there were hundreds of people dancing on the walkways suspended high above the lobby. No one knew that they were just minutes away from one of the most serious structural failures this country had ever experienced.

As the dancers moved to the big band sound, a loud crack was heard. A split second later, two of the crowded suspended walkways collapsed onto the people below. As people hurried to get out of the way, they were showered with tons of concrete and metal. Despite the heroic efforts of rescue personnel, 114 people died and over 200 were injured. When the investigation began, it quickly became apparent that there was a major flaw in the design of the walkways.

The original design called for two of the walkways to be hung with a 50-foot rod extending from the ceiling and through both walkways. In this design, the weight of both walkways was carried to the ceiling because points A and B each held up one walkway.

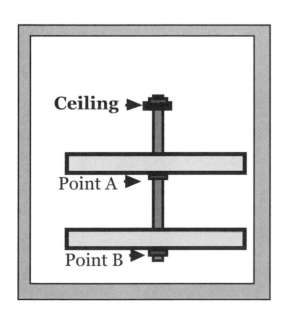

You can think of this design as similar to three people climbing a rope in gym class. Each person holds himself on the rope, and all the weight goes to the ceiling.

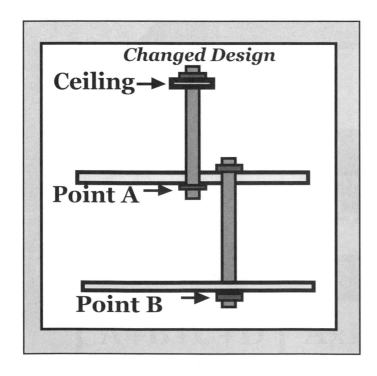

Changed Design

Ceiling →

Point A →

Point B →

Unfortunately, somebody saw the 50-foot rod in the design for the walkway and decided that two 25-foot rods would be much easier to work with. And of course, everyone knows that two 25-foot rods are the same as one 50-foot rod. At first glance it might seem that way, but it is not the same in this situation. No longer is all the weight going to the ceiling. Now, point A not only has to hold up its own walkway, but you can see from the diagram that point A is also holding up the walkway that is below it. Point A was never designed to hold the weight of two walkways. The changed design was much easier to assemble, but it led to the catastrophic collapse.

You can think of this design as similar to three people climbing a rope in gym class. But instead of each person holding the rope, each person holds on to the legs of the person that is higher up. In this situation, all the weight goes to the ceiling, but the top person's hand is holding the weight of three people.

Because point A was forced to support the weight of two concrete walkways and the additional weight of scores of people, it failed.

The human mind is such a powerful problem solver that its susceptibility to being fooled is often overlooked. If a 50-foot rod is a problem, we can use two 25-foot rods. It is easy looking back to see that this is a mistake, but at the time, it was overlooked by the architectural firm and the engineers.

As you attempt the problems on the following pages, remember that the answer that seems obvious is probably wrong. **Think carefully!**

Level 1

1) A dog and a cat together cost $100. If the price of the dog is $90 more than the cat, what is the cost of the cat?

2) $1^{10} =$

3) A 50-pound bowling ball and an 8-pound bowling bowl are dropped from a tall building. Which ball will hit first?

4) Which number is larger?   1.00987   or   1.01

5) A car is traveling on a freeway at 50 mph with the cruise control set at 50 mph. Another car is traveling at 90 mph with the cruise control set at 90 mph. Which car has a higher acceleration?

Level 2

1) Solve: $100 \div 1/2$

2) How many square inches are in a square foot?

3) $5^0 =$

4) A bookstore was selling books for 50% off. A shelf in the store had a sign as shown:

Books on this shelf take an additional 25% off.

Leta picked out books from the discount shelf that had a regular price of $100. How much did Leta pay for the discounted books?

5) It takes Spot 2 hours to paint a fence and Steven 4 hours to paint the same fence. If they work together, how long will it take them to paint the fence?

Level 3

1) Warren was making $100,000 per year. His boss said that he was going to cut his salary 25%, but that Warren shouldn't worry because he would be given a 25% raise the next day. How much will Warren's salary be after the 25% cut and 25% raise?

2) How many cubic inches are in a cubic foot?

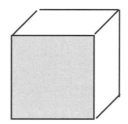

3) If there are 10^{30} grains of sand on Beach A, how many grains of sand are there on a beach that has 10 times the sand as Beach A? (Express your answer using exponents.)

4) Jonathan was thrilled when his boss told him he was going to get a .5% raise. If Jonathan is currently paid $10,000 per year, how much of a raise will he get?

Finally! A good raise. It is about time!

5) If cement cost $4 per cubic foot, how much does a cubic yard of cement cost?

Einstein Level

1) On her 10 mile trip to school, Jessica's car gets 50 mpg of gas. On her way home, her car gets 40 miles per gallon. How many miles per gallon does Jessica's car get during the entire 20 mile trip?

2) Adam drove the 10 miles to school at a speed of 60 mph. On his way home, due to traffic, his speed was 30 mph. What was his average speed for the round trip to school and back?

3) Some scientists believe that there are 10^{87} atoms in the entire universe. The number googolplex is a 1 followed by a googol of zeros. If each atom in the universe is used as a zero, how many universes would you need in order to have enough zeros to write out completely the number googolplex?

4) Alex rode his bike to school at a speed of 12 mph. He then walked home at a speed of 5 mph. What was Alex's average speed for his trip to school and back?

5) When Esteban left for college, his parents decided to give him an allowance of $100 every 4 weeks. They told Esteban that he could decide how he wanted raises to his allowance determined.

Choice #1-----------A raise of $10 every 4 weeks
Choice #2----------A raise of $1.50 each week

Which choice should Esteban pick?

Super Einstein

A wise knight came to a bridge that spanned a deep gorge. The bridge was guarded by an angry mathematician who required the correct answer to a probability problem before the knight would be allowed to pass. The knight accepted the challenge even though the penalty for a wrong answer was clear from the pile of knights at the bottom of the gorge.

The three boxes before you each contain two talking frogs. In one box are two frogs that always lie. Another box contains two frogs that always tell the truth. The remaining box contains one frog that always lies and one frog that always tells the truth.

The knight was then told to pick a box and then take one frog out of the box. The knight then picked a truth-telling frog from the box he chose.

What is the probability that the remaining frog in the box is also a truth-teller?

The Eccentric Mathematician

You are about to take part in a contest that will allow you to enter the Elite Einstein Club. Entering the club is very difficult because you must first climb the five steps of mathematical misery.

At each step you are to determine whether the left side is larger, the right side is larger, they are the same, or there is no way to tell. I have done the first group of steps for you on the next page. In case you are wondering, I will only reveal my identity after you have completed all of the contests. Good Luck!

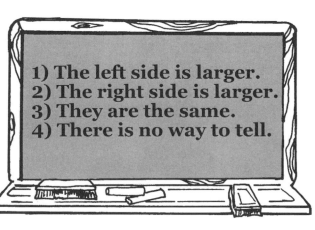

1) The left side is larger.
2) The right side is larger.
3) They are the same.
4) There is no way to tell.

The Eccentric Mathematician
Practice Contest

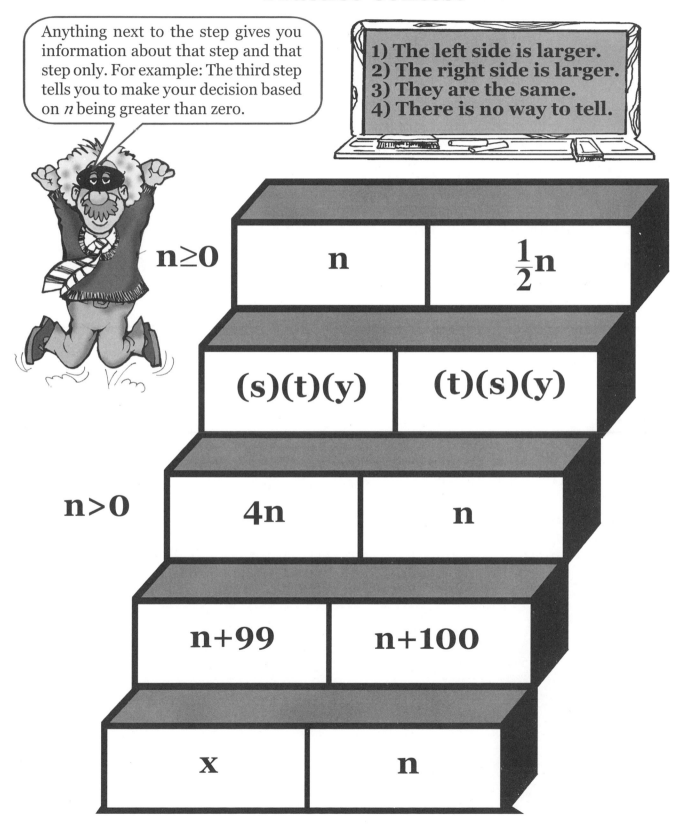

Anything next to the step gives you information about that step and that step only. For example: The third step tells you to make your decision based on *n* being greater than zero.

1) The left side is larger.
2) The right side is larger.
3) They are the same.
4) There is no way to tell.

$n \geq 0$ n $\frac{1}{2}n$

$(s)(t)(y)$ $(t)(s)(y)$

$n > 0$ $4n$ n

$n+99$ $n+100$

x n

The Eccentric Mathematician
Practice Contest Answers

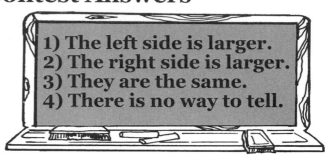

1) The left side is larger.
2) The right side is larger.
3) They are the same.
4) There is no way to tell.

Bottom step: There is no way to tell

x and n could be the same number, or one could be small and the other large.

2nd step: The right side is always larger

The right side is always one larger than the left side.

3rd step: The left side is always larger

As long as n is greater than zero, 4n is always larger than n.

4th step: They are the same

When you rearrange the order of a multiplication problem, the answer is always the same. (The commutative property of multiplication)

5th step: There is no way to tell

If n is zero, they are the same. If n is a positive number, n is always greater than $\frac{1}{2}n$, so you cannot tell which side is greater.

The Eccentric Mathematician
Contest 1

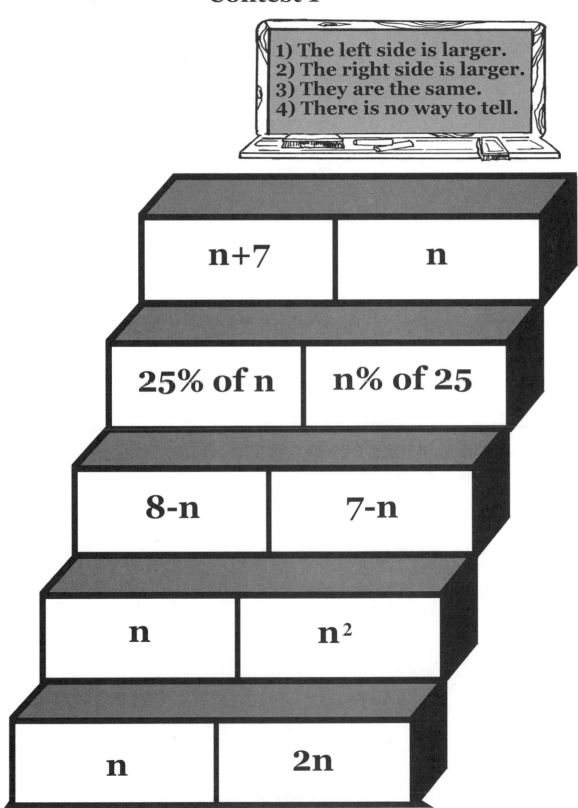

1) The left side is larger.
2) The right side is larger.
3) They are the same.
4) There is no way to tell.

n+7	n
25% of n	n% of 25
8-n	7-n
n	n²
n	2n

The Eccentric Mathematician
Contest 2

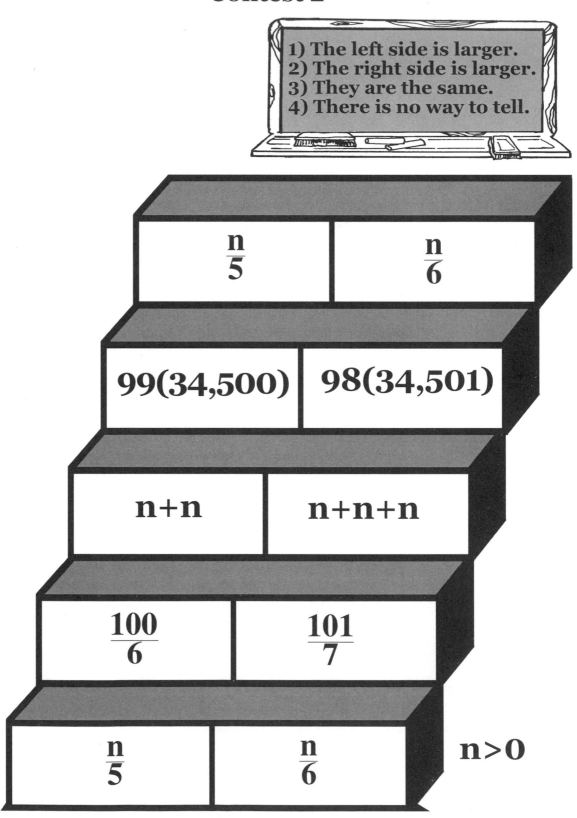

1) The left side is larger.
2) The right side is larger.
3) They are the same.
4) There is no way to tell.

$\dfrac{n}{5}$	$\dfrac{n}{6}$
99(34,500)	**98(34,501)**
n+n	**n+n+n**
$\dfrac{100}{6}$	$\dfrac{101}{7}$
$\dfrac{n}{5}$	$\dfrac{n}{6}$

n>0

The Eccentric Mathematician
Contest 3

1) The left side is larger.
2) The right side is larger.
3) They are the same.
4) There is no way to tell.

Lines all go through the center of the circle.

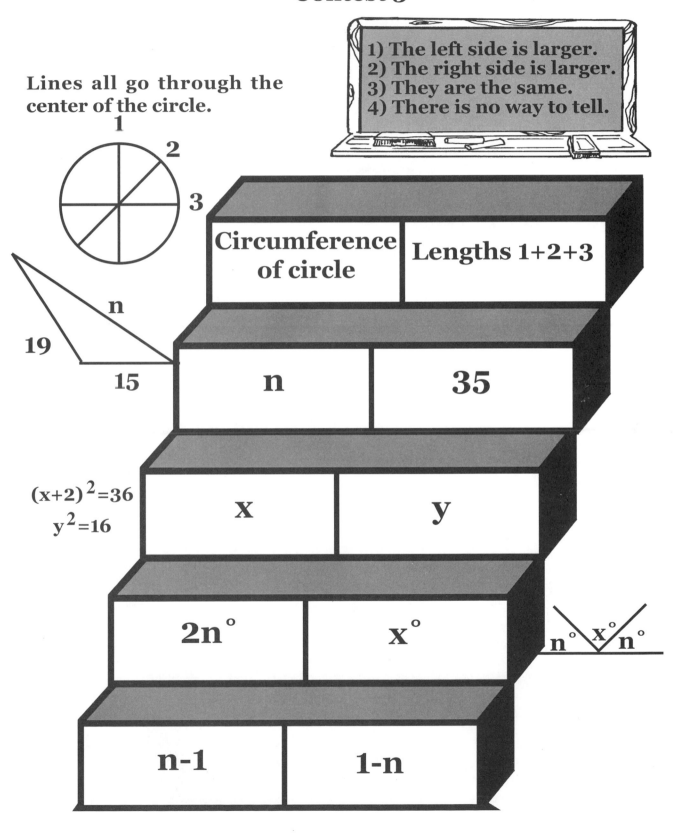

| Circumference of circle | Lengths 1+2+3 |

| n | 35 |

$(x+2)^2=36$
$y^2=16$

| x | y |

| 2n° | x° |

| n-1 | 1-n |

The Eccentric Mathematician
Contest 4

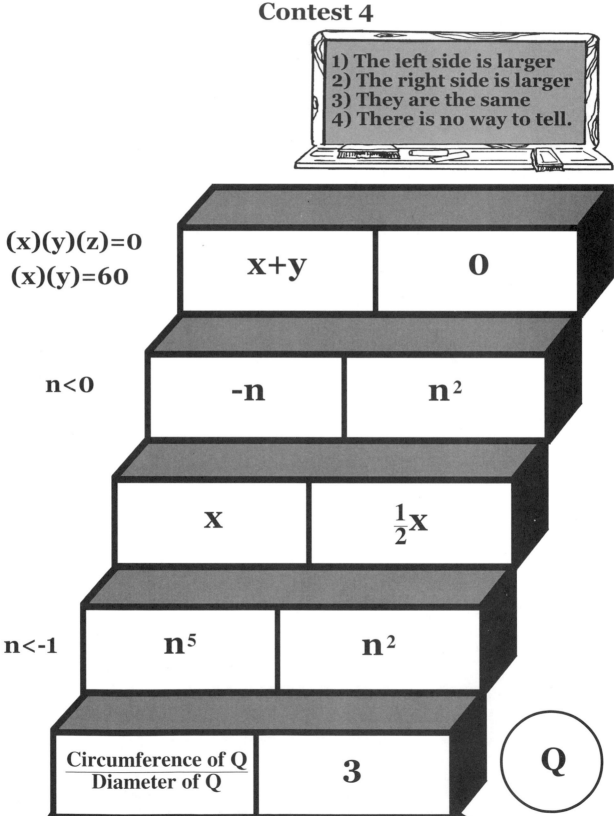

1) The left side is larger
2) The right side is larger
3) They are the same
4) There is no way to tell.

$(x)(y)(z)=0$
$(x)(y)=60$

| $x+y$ | 0 |

$n<0$

| $-n$ | n^2 |

| x | $\frac{1}{2}x$ |

$n<-1$

| n^5 | n^2 |

| $\dfrac{\text{Circumference of Q}}{\text{Diameter of Q}}$ | 3 | Q |

The Eccentric Mathematician
Contest 5

1) The left side is larger.
2) The right side is larger.
3) They are the same.
4) There is no way to tell.

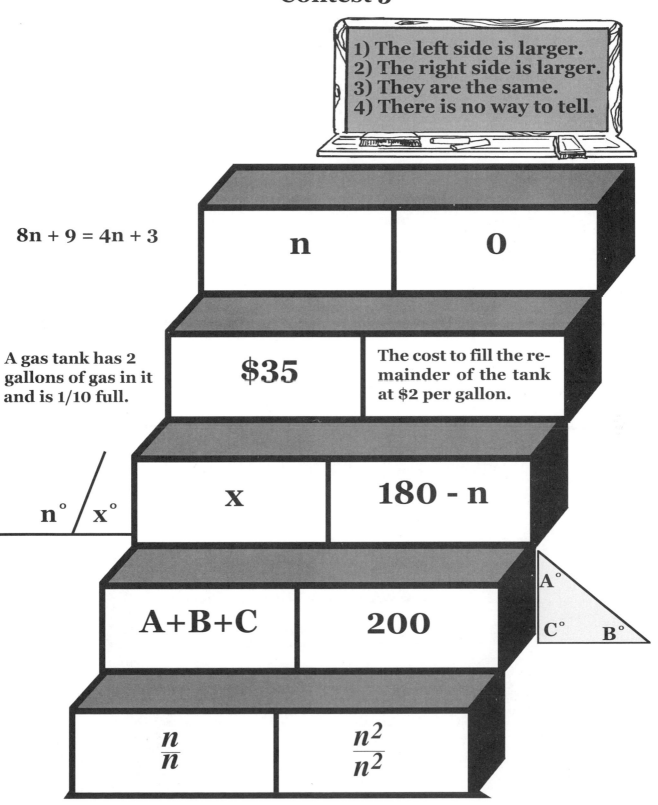

$8n + 9 = 4n + 3$ **n**   **0**

A gas tank has 2 gallons of gas in it and is 1/10 full.   **$35**   The cost to fill the remainder of the tank at $2 per gallon.

$n°\!/x°$ **x**   **180 - n**

A+B+C   **200**

$\dfrac{n}{n}$ $\dfrac{n^2}{n^2}$

The Eccentric Mathematician
Contest 6

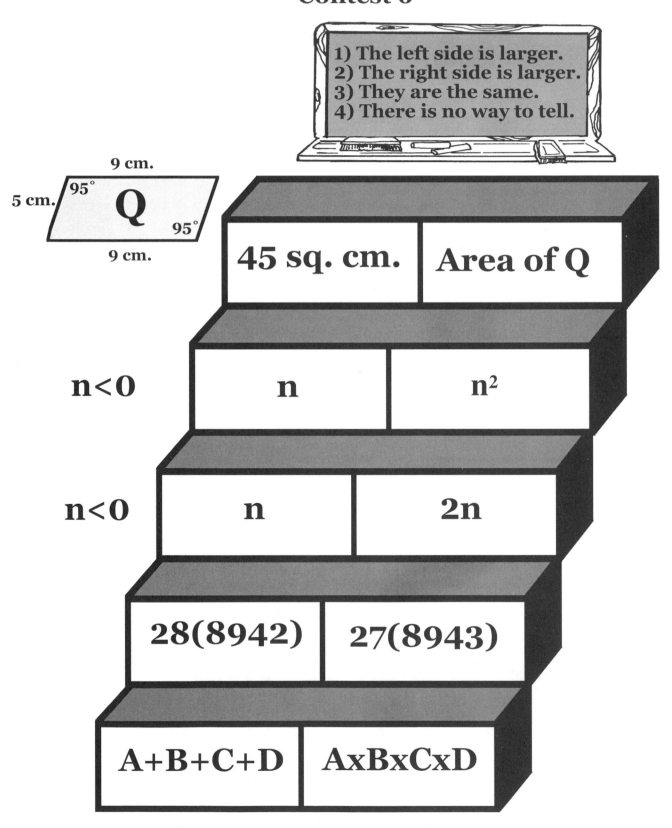

1) The left side is larger.
2) The right side is larger.
3) They are the same.
4) There is no way to tell.

9 cm.

5 cm. 95° **Q**
                        95°
9 cm.

| 45 sq. cm. | Area of Q |

n<0

| n | n² |

n<0

| n | 2n |

| 28(8942) | 27(8943) |

| A+B+C+D | AxBxCxD |

Permutations

Kinta has three pieces of artwork that he wants to hang on three hooks that are on his wall. On Monday he hung the pictures as shown below.

On Tuesday he hung the pictures in a different way.

Kinta kept changing the arrangement of the pictures each day until Sunday when he could not think of a new way to arrange the pictures and had to repeat an arrangement.

Wednesday's arrangement:

Thursday's arrangement:

Friday's arrangement:

Saturday's arrangement:

Sunday---No new arrangement possible!

Kinta easily found how many different ways there are to hang three pictures. What if he has eight pictures? Is there an easy way to find how many arrangements there are for eight pictures?

Yes there is! I am going to teach you a fancy word and a new kind of math notation that looks scary, but is really easy to understand if you relax and don't panic.

When you arrange items in an order, like Kinta did with the paintings, each different arrangement is called a permutation.

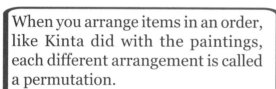

So the number of permutations of 3 paintings is 6. That seems pretty easy.

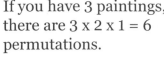

If you have 3 paintings, there are 3 x 2 x 1 = 6 permutations.

$$3 \times 2 \times 1 = 6$$

3 x 2 x 1 can be written as 3! Even though this looks like 3 explanation mark, the correct way to say it is 3 factorial.

If you have 4 paintings, there are 4 x 3 x 2 x 1 = 24 permutations.

$$4 \times 3 \times 2 \times 1 = 24$$

Which of course means that there are 24 ways to arrange the 4 paintings. This seems pretty easy!!

If you have 5 paintings, there are 5 x 4 x 3 x 2 x 1 = 120 permutations

5 x 4 x3 x 2 x 1 = 120

Remember that 5 x 4 x 3 x 2 x 1 can be written as 5!

I see what is happening. If I have 8 paintings, I can arrange them in 8! different ways.

8 x 7 x 6 x 5 x 4 x 3 x 2 x 1 = 40,320

Wow! 8 paintings can be hung in 40,320 different arrangements.

Find how many permutations there are in the problems below. I will be back when you are done.

1) Find the number of permutations of 5 children and 5 desks.

2) Each day Jay brings a lunch that consists of a sandwich, an apple, a candy bar, and a carrot. Jay wants to change the order in which he eats the four items. How many permutations are there for the four items?

3) How many permutations are there for the letters in the word CAT? How many are words?

4) A classroom has 10 students and 10 desks. The teacher decided that each day there would be a different way the children arranged themselves at the desks. How many days would pass before the group of 10 students must repeat an arrangement?

I hope you answered the four problems correctly. The answers are on the next page.

Answers

1) 5! or 5 x 4 x 3 x 2 x 1 = 120 different ways

2) 4! or 4 x 3 x 2 x 1 = 24

3) 3! or 3 x 2 x 1 = 6   <u>cat</u>, cta, <u>tac</u>, tca, <u>act</u>, atc   Three are real words

4) 10! or 10 x 9 x 8 x 7 x 6 x 5 x 4 x 3 x 2 x 1 = 3,628,800

There is a fancy mathematical way to write what we are doing. If we have 5 paintings and 5 hooks, then we are finding the number of permutations of 5 paintings taken 5 at a time.

Watch how I write the permutations of 5 items taken 5 at a time.

$_5P_5$

This brings us to another very interesting type of problem. Look on the blackboard and see how you think you would write the problem.

If you have 5 paintings and only two hooks, how many different ways are there to hang the paintings?

I know what that means. It is 5 things taken 2 at a time. Now I will make a list and see how many ways there are to group two painting when you have 5 paintings.

In this problem you have 5 items, but you are only taking 2 at a time. Look at the fancy way that I write the problem.

$_5P_2$

The answer is 20. That problem was pretty easy.

I just thought of something. What if you had a problem such as 10 paintings and 3 hooks? That kind of problem would take forever to solve. Do I have to write down each group or is there an easier way to do these problems?

There is a very easy way to solve these problems. First write down the fancy math for 10 paintings taken 10 at a time.

$_{10}P_{10}$

Now I need to know how many permutations there are of 8 paintings taken 5 at a time. First I'll write the problem in the fancy math notation.

Remember that the next step is to write out 8 paintings taken 8 at a time.

$_8P_5$

That is very easy. Now I will circle the first 5 numbers because I am taking 5 paintings at a time.

$$_8P_8 = 8 \times 7 \times 6 \times 5 \times 4 \times 3 \times 2 \times 1$$

$$_8P_5 = 8 \times 7 \times 6 \times 5 \times 4 \times 3 \times 2 \times 1$$

You found that there are 6,720 arrangemmments of 8 paintings taken 5 at a time. That was easy!

$$8 \times 7 \times 6 \times 5 \times 4 = 6720$$

Find how many permutations there are in the problems below.

1) An artist had 7 paintings and 2 hooks. How many different ways can the artist hang 7 paintings if she only hangs 2 at a time?

2) Find the answer: $_{12}P_3$

3) How many ways can 20 children sit in 5 chairs?

Answers

1) 42 $_7P_2$ $\boxed{(7 \times 6)}$ x 5 x 4 x 3 x 2 x 1 = 42

2) 1320 $_{12}P_3$ $\boxed{(12 \times 11 \times 10)}$ x 9 x 8 x 7 x 6 x 5 x 4 x 3 x 2 x 1 = 1320

3) 1,860,480 $_{20}P_5$ $\boxed{(20 \times 19 \times 18 \times 17 \times 16 \text{...})}$...............= 1,860,480

Combinations

There is one more type of problem you need to learn how to solve. Look at the problem on the blackboard.

In a classroom of 5 children, the teacher wants 2 volunteers to go to the office. How many different groups can be formed from the class of 5 children?

Steve **Amanda** **Maya** **Michelle** **Don**

Look at the group of Maya and Don. If this was about ways to hang paintings, then **Don-Maya** and **Maya-Don** would be two different groups.

I can see that this situation is not the same as the different ways to hang paintings. What am I going to do?

Maya **Don**
Don **Maya**

Oh I see. **Maya--Don** and **Don-Maya** are really only one group. We have to make sure that we don't count them twice.

To solve problems like these where the order does not matter, first find how many permutations there are.

Okay, that seems easy. There are 5 children taken 2 at a time. There are 20 permutations.

$$_5P_2 = \boxed{5 \times 4} \times 3 \times 2 \times 1 = 20$$

Now we want to get rid of the groups that are the same except for order. We can do this by dividing by $_2P_2$

$$\frac{_5P_2}{_2P_2} = \frac{20}{2} \quad \textbf{10 combinations}$$

Let's try one more problem. Remember that you first find all the permutations and then get rid of the groups that are the same except for order.

In a classroom of 8 children, the teacher wants 3 volunteers to go to the office. How many different groups can be formed from the class of 8 children?

The first step is to find the permutations of 8 children taken 3 at a time.

$$_8P_3 = 8 \times 7 \times 6 \times 5 \times 4 \times 3 \times 2 \times 1 = 336$$

Now I need to get rid of the groups that are the same except for the order they are in.

$$\frac{_8P_3}{_3P_3} = \frac{336}{6}$$ **56 combinations**

1) A class of 25 students will select 4 student council members. How many different combinations arc there in a class of 25 students?

2) Alberto has 10 books that he wants to read. He will only be able to bring 3 books with him during his vacation. How many different groups of 3 books can Alberto pick?

3) Eight jurors will be picked from a jury pool of 30 people. How many possible combinations are there?

Answers

1) 12,650

$_{25}P_4$ 25 x 24 x 23 x 22 = 303,600   Now divide by $_4P_4$ to get rid of groups

that are the same except for order. $\dfrac{_{25}P_4}{_4P_4} = \dfrac{303,600}{24} = 12,650$

2) 120

$_{10}P_3$ 10 x 9 x 8 = 720   Now divide by $_3P_3$ to get rid of groups

that are the same except for order. $\dfrac{_{10}P_3}{_3P_3} = \dfrac{720}{6} = 120$

3) 5,852,925

$_{30}P_8$ 30 x 29 x 28 x 27 x 26 x 25 x 24 x 23 = 235,989,936,000.

Now divide by $_8P_8$ to get rid of groups that are the same except for order.

$\dfrac{_{30}P_8}{_8P_8} = \dfrac{235,989,936,000}{40,320} = 5,852,925$

Level 1

1) Laura has three errands to complete. She must wash the dishes, mow the lawn, and paint a fence. How many ways can Laura arrange the order of the three errands?

2) Abbey knew that the combination for her locker had the numbers 36, 12, 8, and 40, but she couldn't remember the right order of the numbers. How many different possibilities are there for the lock combination using the four numbers?

3) A soccer team has picked its five best players to take part in penalty kicks to determine the winner of a soccer match that is tied. Each of the five players will get one shot against the opposing team's goalie. The coach needs to decide the order in which the five players will take their shots. How many possible ways are there to arrange the five players?

4) Sara wants to arrange the seven scrabble letters she has in every possible way so she can determine if she has a 7-letter word. How many different ways are there for Sara to arrange all seven letters?

5) How many possible batting orders are there for a baseball team with 9 players?

Level 2

1) Ten people are competing for the title of "Best Singer in the World". There will be a 1st place and a 2nd place awarded. How many different ways can the 1st and 2nd place be awarded?

2) Jay has 5 paintings that he plans to display on a wall that only has 4 hooks. Nancy has 5 paintings that she plans to display on a wall with 5 hooks. Who has more possible ways to hang his/her paintings?

3) A mathematician had 8 favorite paintings and only 6 wall hooks to hang the paintings. How many different ways can she hang the paintings?

4) Mrs. Lopez gave a homework assignment over summer vacation to read three books from the following list:

a) Call of the Wild
b) Wuthering Heights
c) Death of a Salesman
d) The Cartoon Book of Physics

How many possible combinations of three books are there in the list of four books?

5) Twelve friends went to a movie theater. Because the movie was boring, they decided to figure out how many different ways they could sit in the 12 seats. How many different permutations are there for these 12 friends?

Level 3

1) A music camp with 50 students decided to break the students into barbershop quartets to see which combination of four students sounded the best. How many different barbershop quartets can be made with 50 students so that each possible combination of four is tried?

2) After a long journey, Samantha finally reached the door to the cave that contained the treasure she had been seeking for over 20 years. The only way to open the door was to place 7 colored spherical objects into their correct places on the cave door.

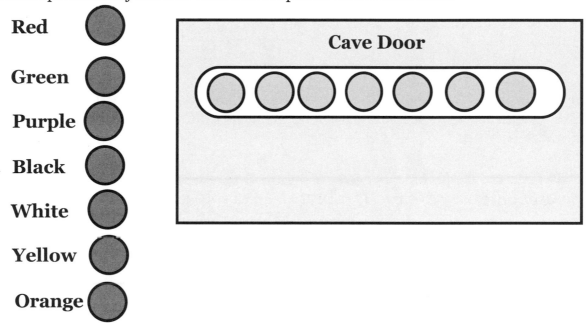

If Samantha started at 12:00 noon and took 15 seconds to place each different arrangement into the door, at what time would she complete all possible permutations?

3) Eight people have volunteered for a secret mission that requires only 3 people. How many different combinations are possible?

4) Five players are going to be picked to start a basketball game. If there are 13 players on the team, how many different combinations of 5 starting players can be made?

5) If 100 people are required to introduce themselves to each other and shake hands with each person one time, how many handshakes will take place?

Einstein Level

1) Seth is constantly forgetting the combination to his lock. He has a lock with four dials. (Each has 10 numbers: 0-9). If Seth can try one lock combination per second, how many seconds will it take him to try every possible lock combination?

2) Lindsey was given a charm bracelet with spaces for four charms before her first day of 1st grade. Along with this bracelet, she was given 15 charms from which to chose four each day for her bracelet.

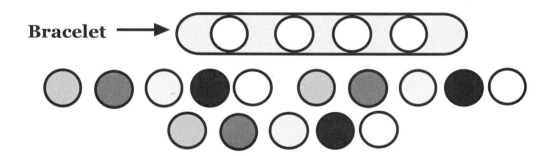

Each day before she would go to school, Lindsey makes sure that she picks a set of four charms that she has never grouped together before. (For example: If Lindsey wore charms 1,2,3, and 4, she could never wear those charms together again.)

If Lindsey goes to school 180 days per year, in what grade will she have used up all the different combinations of charms for her bracelet?

3) One thousand people in a room decide to shake hands with every other person in the room. Instead of one handshake per couple, each person must shake both of the hands of every person in the room with both his right hand and his left hand. (Tom will use his right hand to shake Dave's right hand and then Dave's left hand. Tom will then use his left hand to shake Dave's right hand and then Dave's left hand.) How many total handshakes will take place?

4) An eccentric millionaire has 5 golden hooks from which to hang her expensive artwork. She wants to have enough paintings so she can change the order of the arrangement each day for the next 41 years. (The same five paintings are okay as long as the hanging order is different.) What is the fewest number of paintings she can buy and still have a different arrangement every day for the next 41 years?

5) A baseball team has 25 total players consisting of 15 position players and 10 pitchers. How many different ways are there to arrange the batting order of 9 starting players if only one pitcher is used at a time and the pitcher always bats last.

(This means that 8 players are taken from the position players and one pitcher is then added at the end of the lineup.)

Super Einstein

Samantha's twin sister was searching for a cave with treasure. The cave door she found had 7 colored spherical objects, but the door had 9 spots to place the 7 colored spherical objects. The only way to open the door was to place the 7 colored spherical objects into their correct places on the cave door. If Samantha's sister started on January 1st at 12:00 A.M. (midnight) and took 15 seconds to place each different arrangement into the door, on what date and at what time would she complete all possible permutations?

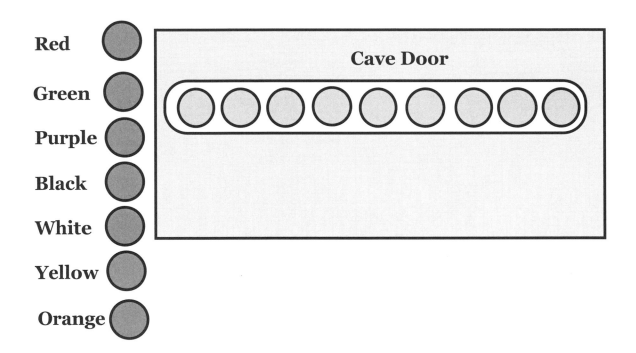

Understanding Bases

I desperately need your help! I am making a science fiction movie about a planet called Septon where they use base 7 instead of our base 10.

I suppose you want me to show you how to count in base 7.

To tell you the truth, I don't even remember what bases are.

Before we talk about base 7, let's review how base 10 works.

Base 10:
What does it mean?

Take the number 6,435.
This means that we have...

5 ones or 5 x 1 = 5

3 tens or 3 x 10 = 30

4 hundreds or 4 x 100 = 400

6 thousands or 6 x 1000 = 6000

Thousands	Hundreds	Tens	Ones
6	4	3	5

6000 + 400 + 30 + 5 = 6,435

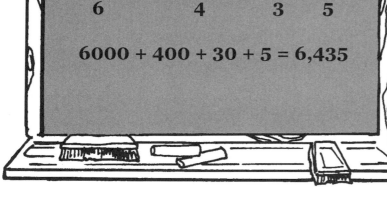

10,000	1,000	100	10	1
	6	4	3	5

I see how you found each column. Because we are in base 10, we can find each column by multiplying by 10.

When you are working in base seven, you need to change the columns. Instead of multiplying by 10 each time, you multiply by 7.

2401	343	49	7	1

If a person from Septon says that hc has 452 donuts, hc doesn't have as many as you might think.

Oh I see! 452 in base 7 is the same as:
2 groups of 1 **(2)**
5 groups of 7 **(35)**
4 groups of 49 **(196)**

2401	343	49	7	1
		4	5	2

That's right! The person from Septon would have 2 + 35 + 196 = 233 donuts.

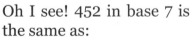

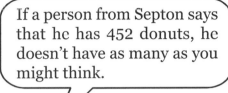

Watch how I change each base 7 number to base 10.

21 (Base 7)

1 group of 1 = 1
2 groups of 7 = 14

1 + 14 = 15

2401	343	49	7	1
			2	1

3002 (Base 7)

2 groups of 1 = 2
0 groups of 7 = 0
0 groups of 49 = 0
3 groups of 343 = 1029

2 + 1029 = 1031

2401	343	49	7	1
	3	0	0	2

54320 (Base 7)

0 groups of 1 = 0
2 groups of 7 = 14
3 groups of 49 = 147
4 groups of 343 = 1372
5 groups of 2401 = 12,005

0 + 14 + 147 + 1372 + 12,005 = 13,538

2401	343	49	7	1
5	4	3	2	0

Try changing these base 7 numbers into base 10. Good luck!

1. **35**
2. **660**
3. **10**
4. **6**
5. **111**

Answers

1) 26
     3 groups of 7 = 21
     5 in one's column = 5   21 + 5 = 26

2) 336
     6 groups of 49 = 294
     6 groups of 7 = 42
     0 in one's column = 0   294 + 42 = 336

3) 7
     1 group of 7 = 7

4) 6
     6 in one's column = 6

5) 57
     1 group of 49 = 49
     1 group of 7 = 7
     1 in one's column = 1   49 + 7 + 1 = 57

Changing base 10 numbers to base 7 is a little tricky. Take the base 10 number **27** for example. Are there any groups of 2401 in 27?

Of course not, 27 is a small number!

27   (Base 10)

Okay, then we will put a 0 in the 2401 column. Are there any groups of 343 or groups of 49 in the base 10 number 27?

No, 27 is smaller than 49 and 343. I see! We need to put zeros in those columns too.

2401	343	49	7	1
0	0	0	3	6

Are there any groups of 7 in the number 27? If so, how many and how many are left over?

There are three groups of 7 in 27 with 6 left over. So a 3 goes in the 7's column and a 6 goes in the one's column.

Because there are 3 groups of 7 and 6 left over, the number 27 is written in base 7 as 36.

2401	343	49	7	1
		0	3	6

That is a lot easier than I thought it would be! Watch how I change the number 100 in base 10 into base 7!

2401	343	49	7	1
		2	0	2

Step 1: There are 2 groups of 49 in 100 with 2 left over.

Step 2: There are no groups of 7 in the 2 that are left over.

Step 3: The 2 that are left over are now placed in the one's column.

Great work! Watch how I change these base 10 numbers into base 7.

2401	343	49	7	1

Base 10   ## Base 7

15   2 groups of 7 (1 left over) ⟶ 21
        plus
        1 left over

53   1 group of 49 (4 left over) ⟶ 104
        0 groups of 7
        4 groups of 1

350   1 groups of 343 (7 left over)
        0 groups of 49   ⟶ 1010
        1 group of 7 (None left over)
        0 groups of 1

Try changing these base 10 numbers into base 7.

1) **9**
2) **25**
3) **130**
4) **6**
5) **2402**

Answers

1) 12

> 1 group of 7 can be taken from 9
>> with
>
> 2 left over for the one's column

2401	343	49	7	1
		0	1	2

2) 34

> 3 groups of 7 can be taken from 25
>> with
>
> 4 left over for the one's column

2401	343	49	7	1
		0	3	4

3) 244

> 2 groups of 49 can be taken from 130
>> with 130 - 98 = 32 left over
>
> 4 groups of 7 can be taken from 32
>> with
>
> 4 left over for the one's column

2401	343	49	7	1
		2	4	4

4) 6

> 6 ones

5) 10001

> 1 group of 2401 can be taken from 2402
>> with
>
> No groups of 343, 49, or 7 left over
>
> 1 is left over for the one's column

2401	343	49	7	1
1	0	0	0	1

Level 1

1) A Septon said that he had 100 rocks. How many rocks does he have in base 10?

2) A Septon said that he has 3 eyes. Does that mean he really has 3 eyes in base 10?

3) A Septon who visited Earth used an Earth scale and found that he weighed 125 pounds. He is horrified that he lost so much weight. Translate 125 pounds base 10 into base 7.

4) How many fingers would you guess a Septon has?

5) What is the base 10 number 100 in base 7?

Level 2

1) Fill in the missing columns for base 2.

?	?	?	?	16	8	4	2	1

2) Change the base 10 number of 25 into base 2.

Computers use base 2. This is my favorite base so be very careful when you do these problems.

3) Change the base 2 number 1000 into base 10.

4) Write the first 9 columns for base 5.

?	?	?	?	?	?	?	?	?

5) Change the base 10 number 100 into base 5.

Level 3

1) A Septon said that he has a collection of 1,000,000 stones in his house. How many stones is that in base 10?

2) If someone has $1,000,000 in base 2, how much money does she have in base 10?

3) If a person from Septon ate .1 of their cookie, what fraction of the cookie did they eat using base 10?

4) In base 10 the number 25.12 actually means 20 + 5 + 1/10 + 2/100. What does the base 7 number 25.12 mean?

5) A Septonian said he had eaten .5 of his cookie while an American said he had eaten .5 of his cookie. Who ate more? Why?

Einstein
Level

1) In base 10, the number .111111... approaches 1/9. What does .11111111 base 2 approach in base 10?

2) A Septonian won the lottery in the United States and won $1,000,000. How many dollars is that in base 7?

3) A Septonian said that his exact weight is 250.346 pounds (base 7). Translate this into base 10.

Use the following story for problems 4 and 5:
A visitor from the planet Badluckton needs to learn the counting system that is used on Earth. He is having a problem because Badlucktonians use a base 13 counting system while people on Earth use a base 10 counting system. In addition, a number of people from Earth are going to visit Badluckton and need to learn how to work in a base 13 system.

We will need to design 3 new digits for base 13:
10...........#
11............&
12...........*

4) If each Badlucktonian has 13 fingers, how would they express that number in base 13?

5) Change the base 10 number 1000 into base 13.

Super Einstein

A Badluckton says that it takes *&# days for her planet to orbit her sun. How many days would that be in a base 10 system? (Use the information from Einstein Level problems numbers 4 and 5.)

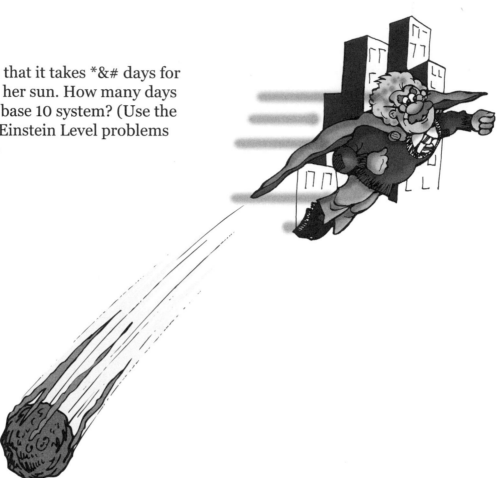

Who Wants to be a Googolillionaire?

$Million	What is $33\frac{1}{3}\%$ of 9?
$Billion	What is the formula for the area of a circle?
$Trillion	What is the formula for the circumference of a circle?
$Quadrillion	How many millimeters are in a meter?
$Quintillion	How many square feet are in a square yard?
$Sextillion	What is the weight of a liter of water expressed in kilograms?
$Septillion	Change 1/9 to a decimal.
$Octillion	A 3-foot stick casts a shadow of 8 feet. If at the same time a tree casts a shadow of 15 feet, how tall is the tree?
$Nonillion	What is the formula for the volume of a cylinder?
$Decillion	If Distance equals Speed times Time (D=SxT), then what does time equal in terms of speed and distance?
$Undecillion	A metal block is made of nickel and copper. The weight of the metals in the block are in a ratio of 2:9. The weight of the block is 407 pounds. What is the weight of the nickel?
$Duodecillion	A right triangle has legs of 9 feet and 12 feet. How long is the hypotenuse?
$Tredecillion	The tax in a state is 5%. If Eric paid $4.60 tax for a bike, what was the cost of the bike before sales tax was added?
$Quattuordecillion	What is the weight of a cubic meter of water? Express your answer in kilograms.
$Googol	How many microns are in a meter?

Use Calculator	Look in Book	Ask a Friend	Teacher Hint

Lifelines

Who Wants to be a Googolillionaire?

$Million	Write .02 as a percent.
$Billion	Write 7% as a decimal.
$Trillion	What is 65% of 200?
$Quadrillion	A book is discounted 45%. If the original price is $40, what is the new price?
$Quintillion	1/3 + 1/7 =
$Sextillion	$6\frac{1}{8} x \frac{1}{7} =$
$Septillion	A book cost $8.50 without tax. If the tax rate is 7%, what is the total cost of the book including tax?
$Octillion	$18 - 6\frac{1}{9} =$
$Nonillion	$22\frac{1}{2} \div \frac{1}{8} =$
$Decillion	A triangle has an area of 60 square inches and a base of 10 inches. What is its height?
$Undecillion	Compare a decimeter to a meter using percents. (A decimeter is what percent of a meter?)
$Duodecillion	Compare a gallon to a quart using percent. (A gallon is what percent of a quart?)
$Tredecillion	What is the Least Common Multiple of 3,4,5?
$Quattuordecillion	When a circle's radius triples, what happens to its area?
$Googol	A store sells books for 50% off on Sundays. The store advertises that on Easter Sunday the store takes an additional 25% off. What would a pile of books cost on Easter Sunday that normally sell for $100 on a Thursday?

Use Calculator	**Look in Book**	**Ask a Friend**	**Teacher Hint**

Lifelines

Math Contests Level 1

1) If cats cost $15 each. What is the cost of *n* cats?

Please, I beg of you. Do not buy any cats!!

2) The scale of a map shows that 1/2 inch is equal to 3/4 of a mile. How many inches on a map would be equal to 3 miles?

3) There are 30 students in a classroom. Eighteen students read *A Wrinkle in Time* while 22 children read *The Hobbit.* If all children read at least one of the books, how many read both books?

4) If a die is rolled, what is the probability that the number rolled will not be a "5"?

5) How many ways are there to hang 5 paintings on 5 hooks?

Math Contests Level 2

1) A magic box has pennies in it that double every minute. If the box takes an hour to become completely full, how long does it take for the box to become half full?

2) Sara bought a gas-electric hybrid car. She traveled 481.25 miles and used 9.625 gallons of gas. How many miles did the hybrid car travel for each gallon of gas?

3) It took 3.5 gallons of paint to cover a wall that is 985 square feet. How many gallons will it take to cover a wall that is 6501 square feet?

4) The triangle shown below is an isosceles triangle. Find the value of n.

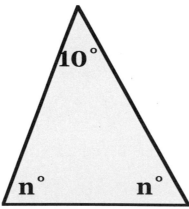

5) Janet would like to put up a straight 100 foot fence. If she places a post every 10 feet, how many posts will she need?

Math Contests Level 3

1) Bill and nine of his friends each have a lot of money in the bank. Bill has 10^{10} dollars in his account, while each of his friends has 10^9 dollars in an account. If all nine of Bill's friends pool their money, who has more money, Bill or his group of nine friends?

2) Dan bought a computer in a state that has a sales tax rate of 7%. If he paid $67.20 sales tax, what did the computer cost?

3) Nancy's car gets n miles per gallon of gas. If she travels x miles, how many gallons of gas did she use?

4) Rachel made a circle graph to show her monthly expenses. If Rachel's monthly expenses were $1080, how much money did she spend on miscellaneous expenses?

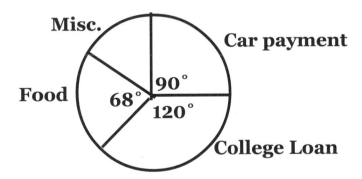

5) The figure ABCD is a square that is divided into 4 squares. The area of the shaded part is 18 square inches. What is the length of each side of the square?

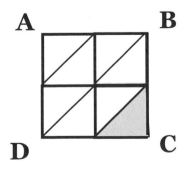

Math Contests Einstein Level

1) B is the center of the circle, which has an area of 314 square feet. If ABCD is a square, what is the length of AC?

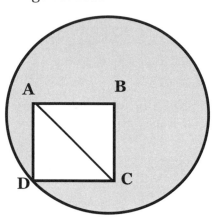

2) A group of people was surveyed to determine what newspaper they read. 80% of those interviewed read the New York Times, while 50% read U.S.A. Today. If 35% read both papers, what percent read neither paper?

3) Anna painted 1/6 of a wall, Eric painted 1/5 of the wall, and Meadow painted 1/4 of the wall. There are now 3910 square feet left to paint. How many square feet did Anna paint?

4) Stacy wanted to make a pie chart to show her monthly expenses. She decided to make the unique chart shown. (The figure within the circle is a square) If Stacy's monthly expenses are $1000, how much does she put into savings each month? (Round to the nearest dollar.)

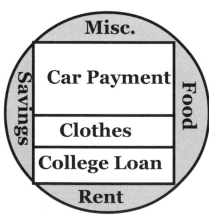

5) Martha can read a 300 page book in 10 hours. How many pages will she read in *n* minutes?

Math Contests Einstein Level

1) How long is side *n*?

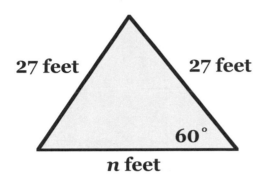

27 feet

27 feet

60°

n feet

2) A class of *n* students was raising money for a field trip. They have earned $800 so far. Each student plans to work *x* more hours at a wage of *y* dollars per hour. When they are done, how much money will they have earned?

3) A rectangular prism has a width of *x* feet, a length of *y* feet, and a height of *h* feet. Express its volume in square inches.

4) AB is the diameter of the large circle and is 10 inches.
   y is the center of the circle.
      What is the area of the shaded part?

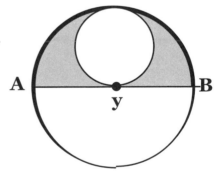

A

B

y

5) A clothing store buys shirts for *n* dollars and then marks them up 50%. To reward their employees, the store gives a 50% discount to all employees. How much does an employee pay for a shirt?

Math Contests Super Einstein Level

1) George and William both ran a one mile race. William won the race with a time of 4 minutes and 30 seconds. If George was 480 feet behind William when the race finished, how long did it take George to run the entire mile? (George continued to run at the same pace.)

2) When five people are playing a game called hearts, each person is dealt ten cards and the two remaining cards are put face down on the table.

Because of the rules of the game, it is very important to know the probability of either of the two cards being a heart. What is the probability that at least one card is a heart?

3) A number of dogs are to equally share a bag of dog food. If there are *n* dogs in the group and one dog eats its share, what percent of the bag is left?

4) Three tennis balls each have a radius of 2 inches. They are put into a 12 inch high cylinder with a 4 inch diameter. What is the volume of the space remaining in the cylinder?

Did you know that the formula for volume of a sphere is 1.33 x pi x r^3?

Think 1

Level 1

1) 10 hours

Think 1:   How long would it take one worker to unload the truck?
5 workers x 12 hours = 60 hours for one worker.

1 worker: 60 hours
2 workers: 60 ÷ 2 = 30 hours
3 workers: 60 ÷ 3 = 20 hours
6 workers: 60 ÷ 6 = 10 hours

2) Yes

Think 1:   How long would the oxygen last one person?
2 people x 6 days = 12 days for one person.

1 astronaut: 12 days
2 astronauts: 6 days
3 astronauts: 12 ÷ 3 = 4 days

3) 3 hours

Think 1:   How long would it take one person to clean the warehouse?
3 people x 4 hours = 12 hours.

1 person: 12 hours
2 people: 6 hours
4 people: 12 hours ÷ 4 = 3 hours

4) 10.5 hours

Think 1:   How long will it take one person to dig the hole?
7 people x 3 hours = 21 hours.

1 person: 21 hours
2 people: 21 ÷ 2 = 10.5 hours

5) 1/7 of the fence

If Deanna takes 7 hours to paint a fence, she is painting 1/7 of the fence per hour.

Level 2

1) 2 hours

Think 1:   What fraction of the lawn can Mike finish with the riding mower in one hour? The answer of course is 1/3 of the lawn.

What fraction of the lawn can Mike's sister finish in one hour? The answer of course is 1/6 of the lawn.

1/3 + 1/6 = 1/2 the lawn in one hour, so it will take them two hours to mow the entire lawn.

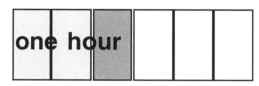

2) 12 days

Think 1:   If one person took all the food, it would last for 6 people x 14 days = 84 days. (Luke and 5 friends add up to 6 people)

1 person: 84 days
2 people: 42 days
7 people: 84 days ÷ 7 people = 12 days

3) 60 days

Think 1:   If one person dug the tunnel all by herself, it would take 12 x 100 = 1200 days.

1 person: 1200 days
2 people: 600 days
20 people: 1200 days ÷ 20 workers = 60 days

4) 12 days

Think 1:   The box will feed one goldfish 3 x 28 days = 84 days.

1 goldfish: 84 days
2 goldfish: 42 days
7 goldfish: 84 days ÷ 7 = 12 days

5) 3 hours

Think 1:   One person can pick all the apples in 3 x 5 hours = 15 hours

1 person: 15 hours
2 people: 7.5 hours
5 people: 15 hours ÷ 5 people = 3 hours

Level 3

1) 2 additional painters

Think 1:   It would take one painter 4 x 12 hours = 48 hours to paint the house.

1 painter: 48 hours
2 painters: 24 hours
n painters: 8 hours   48 hours ÷ 8 hours = 6 painters

2) 1 hour and 20 minutes

Think 1:   Hose A can fill 1/4 of the pool in one hour, while hose B can fill 1/2 of the pool in one hour.

In one hour 1/4 + 1/2 = 3/4 of the pool will be filled.

If 3/4 take 60 minutes, then each of the 3 quarters takes 20 minutes.

3) One hour

Think 1:   Michelle can paint 1/2 of the car in one hour. Tyler can paint 1/3 of the car in one hour. Colton can paint 1/6 of the car in one hour.

1/2 + 1/3 + 1/6 = 1 car in the one hour.

4) 5 minutes and 20 seconds

Think 1:   The time it would take for one child to eat the whole pizza is 4 x 12 minutes = 48 minutes.

1 child: 48 minutes
2 children: 24 minutes
9 children: 48 minutes ÷ 9 children = 5.333 minutes

1/3 of a minute is equal to 20 seconds

5) 30 minutes

Think 1:   In one hour the faucet will fill 5 tubs. In one hour, the drain will empty 3 tubs.

If the combination of water going into the tub and emptying fills two tubs in one hour, then one tub would be filled in 1/2 hour.

Alternative Think 1: The faucet will fill 1/12 of the tub in one minute. The drain will empty 1/20 of the tub in one minute.

In one minute 1/12 - 1/20 = 1/30 of the tub will be filled
(5/60 - 3/60 = 2/60 = 1/30)

If one minute fills 1/30 of the tub, then it will take 30 minutes to fill the tub.

Einstein Level

1) 20 hours

Think 1:   Think one hour. Each hour, 1/4 of the pool is filled, but 1/5 is drained away.

The amount that is left is 1/4 - 1/5 or 5/20 - 4/20 = 1/20

Each hour, 1/20 of the pool is filled, so it will take 20 hours to fill the pool.

2) 4 additional plows

Think 1:   If one plow did all the work, it would take 3 x 14 hours = 42 hours

1 plow: 42 hours
n plows: 6 hours   42 hours ÷ 6 hours = 7 plows total

3) 4 minutes and 48 seconds

Think 1:   How much of the walk can Brandon shovel in one minute? Because he can shovel the whole walk in 8 minutes, he can shovel 1/8 of the walk in one minute.

His brother can shovel 1/12 of the walk in one minute.

Together they can shovel 1/8 + 1/12 = 5/24 of the walk in one minute.

This means that the two brothers can shovel 20/24 of the walk in 4 minutes, with 4/24 of the walk left over.

If 5/24 is equal to 60 seconds, then 1/24 is equal to 60 ÷ 5 = 12 seconds
4/24 must be equal to 4 x 12 = 48 seconds.

4) 5 additional workers

Think 1:   It would have taken one worker 10 x 6 months or 60 months to build the first half of the road, so it would take this single worker 60 months to finish the road.

1 worker: 60 months
2 workers: 30 months
n workers: 4 months   60 months ÷ 4 months = 15 workers

5) 2 hours and 13 1/3 minutes

Think one hour: What fraction of the fence does each paint in one hour?

Anna: 1/4 fence
Brother: 1/5 fence

In one hour, they will paint 1/4 + 1/5 = 9/20 of the fence.
In two hours, they will paint 18/20 of the fence.

Because each hour 9/20 of the fence is painted, each 1/20 of the fence takes 60 ÷ 9 = 6 2/3 minutes.

The remaining 2/20 will take 6 2/3 x 2 = 13 1/3 minutes

Super Einstein

Answer: 32 additional workers

Think 1:   If one worker dug the 3/8 of the tunnel, it would have taken
             8 x 10 = 80 days.

             If 3/8 took 80 days, then each 1/8 of the tunnel would have taken
             the single worker 80 ÷ 3 = 26 2/3 days.

             The remaining 5/8 of the tunnel would take the single worker
             5 x 26 2/3 = 133 1/3 days

1 worker: 133 1/3 days
2 workers: 66 2/3 days
n worker: 3 1/3 days   133 1/3 ÷ 3 1/3 = 40 workers needed

If there are already 8 workers, then an additional 32 are needed.

2-10 Method

Level 1

1) $1.00 per pound

2-10 method: If 2 pounds cost $10, what is the price per pound?
The answer is clearly $5 per pound. How did we arrive at $5 per pound?
The $5 answer was found by dividing. $10 ÷ 2 = $5

Real Problem: $2.50 ÷ $2\frac{1}{2}$ = $1.00

2) $5.76

2-10 method: If cheese cost $2 per pound, what is the cost of 10 pounds of cheese?
The answer is obviously 2 x 10 = $20

Real problem: $2.35 per pound x 2.45 pounds = $5.76

3) 1/6 of a pizza

2-10 method: Kaartek bought 2 pizzas for 10 people. How much pizza should each get?
It is fairly easy to see that the answer is found by dividing the pizzas by the number of people. 2 ÷ 10 = 1/5

Real problem: 86 pizzas ÷ 516 people = 1/6 pizza per person

4) 8 miles

2-10 method: If 2 inches are equal to 10 miles, how many miles is one inch equal to?
It is clear that the answer is 10 ÷ 2 = 5 miles

Real problem: 6 ÷ .75 = 8 miles

5) 4y + 2z

2-10 method: There are 2 horses and 10 chickens in the barn.
The number of legs is easy to find:
2 horses x 4 legs each plus 10 chickens x 2 legs each = 28 legs

Real problem: y horses x 4 legs each + z chickens x 2 legs each = 4y + 2z

Level 2

1) 1600 pieces

2-10 method: How many 2 pound pieces can be cut from a 10 pound meatball?
It is easy to see that the answer is 10 ÷ 2 = 5 pieces.

Real problem: 1200 ÷ 3/4   or   1200 ÷ .75 = 1600 pieces

2) 2/3 pound

2-10 method: If Juan spent $2 for ground beef that cost $10 per pound, how much ground beef did Juan buy?
It is fairly easy to see that he bought 2 ÷ 10 = 1/5 pound

Real problem: 1.28 ÷ 1.92 = 2/3 of a pound

3) xy dollars

2-10 method: If the cost of each hat is 2 dollars, what is the cost of 10 hats?
It is easy to see that the answer is 2 x 10 = $20

Real problem: Multiply: x times y = xy dollars

4) 64 minutes

2-10 method: If Jay reads 2 pages per minute, how long will it take him to read a 10 page book?
It is clear that the answer is 10 ÷ 2 = 5 minutes

Real problem: 72 pages ÷ $1\frac{1}{8}$ pages per minute   72 ÷ 1.125 = 64 minutes

5) 55 miles per hour

2-10 method: A truck driver took 2 hours to travel 10 miles. What was his average speed?
Obvious answer is 10 miles ÷ 2 hours = 5 miles per hour

Real problem: Now we know that this is a division problem.
 426.25 miles ÷ 7.75 hours = 55 miles per hour
(7 hours and 45 minutes is 7.75 hours because 45 minutes is 3/4 of an hour.)

Level 3

1) .8 miles per gallon

2-10 method: A tank used 2 gallons to go 10 miles. How many miles per gallon did the tank travel?
It is fairly easy to see that the 10 miles is split into 2 pieces.
10 miles ÷ 2 gallons = 5 miles for each gallon.

Real problem: Now we know that in order to find our answer we must do miles ÷ gallons.
17.6 miles ÷ 22 gallons = .8 miles per gallon

2) 87.5 red blood cells

2-10 method: 10 red blood cells are created in the bone morrow each second. How many red blood cells would be created in 2 seconds.
It is clear that you must multiply to get the answer: 2 x 10 = 20

Real problem: 2800 blood cells x .03125 seconds = 87.5 blood cells

3) 8 2/5 hours

2-10 method: If it takes 10 hours to paint 2 trucks, how long will it take to paint one truck?
It is easy to see that it will take 5 hours to paint one truck: 10 ÷ 2 = 5 hours

Real problem: 6 hours ÷ 5/7 = 42/5 hours   or $8\dfrac{2}{5}$ hours

4) 3.72 miles

2-10 method: The sound from a thunderstorm travels approximately 2 miles in one second. How far will it travel in 10 seconds?
The answer is clearly found by multiplying: 2 miles x 10 seconds = 20 miles

Real problem: 1/5 mile x 18.6 seconds = 3.72 miles

5) 5(N-Q)

2-10 method: Lamar had 10 (N) albums and he didn't sell 2 (Q) of them. How much money did he make?
It is easy to see that you must subtract (10-2 = sold 8) and then multiply by $5.

Real problem: (N-Q) x $5 = 5(N-Q)

Einstein Level

1) 93 hours and 20 minutes

2-10 method: A 50 gallon water heater leaks 2 gallons of water every 10 minutes. How long until it is completely empty?

When it is written this way, it is fairly easy to see that you must find how many 2-gallon parts there are in 50 gallons.
50 gallons ÷ 2 gallons per minute = 25 parts

Real problem: 50 gallons ÷ .125 gallons per minute = 400 parts

400 parts that each take 14 minutes to drain: 400 x 14 = 5600 minutes

5600 minutes ÷ 60 minutes per hour = 93.33 hours   or 93 hours and 20 minutes.

2) 2000n minutes

2-10 method: A spacecraft with a volume of 800 cubic feet is leaking air at a rate of 2 cubic feet every 10 minutes. How many minutes until the spacecraft has no air?

When it is written this way, it is easy to see that you must find how many 2 cubic foot parts there are in 800 cubic feet. 800 ÷ 2 = 400 parts

400 parts with each taking 10 minutes to leak would take 400 x 10 minutes = 4000 minutes until the spacecraft is empty.

Real problem: 800 cubic feet ÷ .4 cubic feet = 2000 parts

2000 parts x n minutes = 2000n minutes until the spacecraft is empty.

3) 37,474,057.25 meters

2-10 method: A meter is defined as the distance light travels in 2 seconds. How far does light travel in 10 seconds?

It is fairly easy to see that the answer is found by determining how many 2 second sections there are in 10 seconds: 10 seconds ÷ 2 seconds = 5 meters

Real problem: $1/8$ second ÷ $\dfrac{1}{299,792,458}$ seconds = 37,474,057.25 meters

4) t/n hours

2-10 method: Joseph can paint 2 cars in 10 hours. How long does it take him to paint one car?

The answer is clearly 5 hours: 10 hours ÷ 2 cars = 5 hours.

Real problem: t hours ÷ n cars = t/n hours

5) n/60 hours

2-10 method: If a car is traveling at a speed of 2 miles per hour, how many hours will it take for the car to travel 10 miles?

It is clear that if a car goes 2 miles in one hour, it will go 10 miles in 5 hours. We found this by dividing: 10 miles ÷ 2 miles each hour = 5 hours

Real problem: n miles ÷ 60 miles per hour = $\dfrac{n}{60} hours$

Super Einstein

Answer: 2nm/60t

2-10 method: A gasoline tank is leaking at a rate of 10 gallons in 2 hours. If the gasoline cost $2 per gallon, what is the value of the gasoline that will be lost in m minutes?

In this problem, gas is leaking at the rate of 5 gallons per hour: 10 gallons ÷ 2 hours = 5 gallons per hour.

Real problem: n gallons ÷ t hours = $\dfrac{n}{t}$ gallons per hour are leaking.

The value of the gas that is leaking each hour is easy to find because it is $2 per gallon:

$\dfrac{n}{t}$ gallons x $2 for each gallon = 2n/t dollars per hour is the value of the leaking gas.

Now we know that the value of the leaking gas is $\dfrac{2n}{t}$ dollars per hour, but we want per minute. To find the value per minute, simply divide by 60:

$$\frac{2n}{t} \div 60 = \frac{2n}{t} x \frac{1}{60} = \frac{2n}{60t}$$

The value of the leaking gas is $\dfrac{2n}{60t}$ dollars per minute and we have m minutes.

$\dfrac{2n}{60t}$ dollars x m minutes = $\dfrac{2nm}{60t}$ *dollars*

$\dfrac{2nm}{60t}$ *dollars* is the value of the gas that will be lost in m minutes.

Sometimes You Must Subtract

Level 1

1) 120°
A straight line has a total measure of 180°.   180° - 60° = 120°

2) 3/4
The probability that there will be two heads is 1 in 4, so the probability that there will not be two heads is 3 in 4. 1 - 1/4 = 3/4

3) 89°
The measure of the three interior angles of a triangle add up to 180°.
180° - 56° - 35° = 89°

4) 49 square feet
The area of the large rectangle is 5 x 10 = 50 square feet
        The area of the small white rectangle is 1 x 1 = 1 square foot
                50 - 1 = 49 square feet

5) 999,999/1,000,000

1 - 1/1,000,000 = 999,999/1,000,000

Level 2

1) 35/36

There are 36 possible outcomes when two dice are rolled:

1,1	2,1	3,1	4,1	5,1	6,1
1,2	2,2	3,2	4,2	5,2	6,2
1,3	2,3	3,3	4,3	5,3	6,3
1,4	2,4	3,4	4,4	5,4	6,4
1,5	2,5	3,5	4,5	5,5	6,5
1,6	2,6	3,6	4,6	5,6	6,6

Larry's chance of getting double sixes is 1/36, so his chance of not getting double sixes is 35/36.

2) 28 square inches

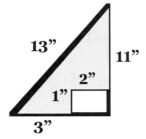

The area of the triangle is 5 x 12 = 60 ÷ 2 = 30 square inches
The area of the small rectangle is 2 square inches
30 square inches - 2 square inches = 28 square inches

3) 80% of Q or .8Q

Q (regular price)
-.2Q (discount)
.8Q

4) 1 - X

Probability always adds up to one.

5) 7.74 square inches

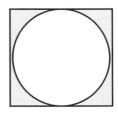

The area of the square is 36 square inches, so each side must be 6 inches long. The diameter of the circle therefore must equal 6 inches. (and the radius 3")

Area of the circle: 3.14 x 3 x 3 = 28.26 square inches
Area of the shaded part:

Area of the square (36) - Area of the circle (28.26) = 7.74 square inches.

Level 3

1) 220°

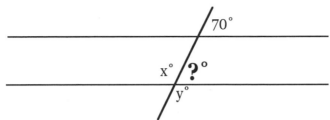

Because the lines are parallel, we know that the angle with the question mark must equal 70°.

Because a straight line is 180°, angle x must equal 180° - 70° = 110°

Because a straight line is 180°, angle y must also equal 110°   x + y = 220°

2) 24 quarts

The area of Fantasia's room can be found by using the formula $A = \pi \, r^2$
Area = 3.14 x 12.5 x 12.5 = 490.625 square feet
The area of the 5-foot diameter circle: 3.14 x 2.5 x 2.5 = 19.625 square feet

We know that each quart of paint covers 19.625 square feet.

The area of the room that still needs to be painted
can be found by subtracting the painted area from
the area of the room: 490.625 - 19.625 = 471 square feet

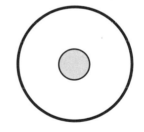

471 square feet ÷ 19.625 square feet (per quart) = 24 quarts

3) 228 square feet

The area of Jonathan's room is 20 x 24 = 480 square feet.
The dimensions of the part of his room that will not be carpeted are 14 feet by 18 feet. (The carpeting is 3 feet wide on each side.) Area is 14 x 18 = 252 square feet

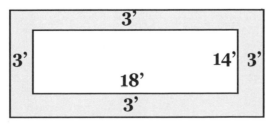

Subtract the area that is not carpeted from the area of the entire room:

480 - 252 = 228 square feet

4) 28.5 square inches

The area of the circle is 3.14 x 10 x 10 = 314 square inches.

The area of 1/4 of the circle is 314 ÷ 4 = 78.5 square inches.

The area of the triangle is 10 x 10 x 1/2 = 50 square inches.

The area of the shaded part is the area of 1/4 of the circle minus the area of the triangle: 78.5 - 50 = 28.5 square inches

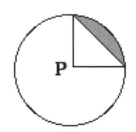

5) 20 square inches

Because the area of the square is 100 square inches, the length of each side of the square is 10 inches.

The base of each of the four white triangles is 8 inches and the height is 5 inches. The area of each triangle then is 8 x 5 x 1/2 = 20 square inches.
The area of the four triangles is 80 square inches.

The area of the shaded part can be found by subtracting the area of the four triangles from the area of the square: 100 - 80 = 20 square inches

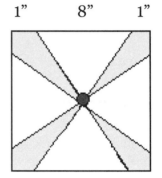

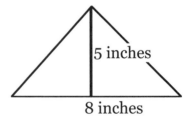

Einstein Level

1) The doctor simply added the percents. If 50% of men snored and 50% of women snored, there would not be a 100% chance of someone snoring when a man and a woman are together.

2) 58.75%

As you pick one man and one woman, you must find the probability that each will not be a snorer.

45% of men snore, so 55% of men do not snore (11/20)
        25% of women snore, so 75% of women do not snore (3/4)

11/20 x 3/4 = 33/80 chance that neither of the two people together are snoring.

If there is a 33/80 chance that neither person is snoring, there is a
1 - 33/80 = 47/80 chance that at least one of the two will be snoring.

$$47 \div 80 = .5875 \text{ or } 58.75\%$$

3) $8.60

The area of the plywood: 4 x 8 = 32 square feet

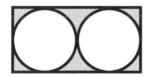

Area of each round top: ($A = \pi \ r^2$)
                3.14 x 2 x 2 = 12.56 square feet

Area of 2 round tops: 2 x 12.56 = 25.12 square feet
The waste is the area of the piece of plywood minus
the area of the two round tops: 32 - 25.12 = 6.88 square feet

The cost per square foot: $40 ÷ 32 square feet = $1.25

6.88 x 1.25 = $8.60

4) 91/216 chance of winning

Most people will say that Janelle has a 3 in 6 chance of winning (1 in 2), but this is incorrect. This incorrect line of thinking would mean Janelle would have a 6 in 6 (100%) chance if she rolled the die 6 times. She obviously would not be assured of winning with six rolls.

To answer this question, you must ask what Janelle's chances of losing are on each roll. The answer of course is 5/6.

Janelle's probability of losing with three rolls is 5/6 x 5/6 x 5/6 = 125/216

Therefore her probability of winning is 1 - 125/216 = 91/216

5) $1500

The value of a year's work is $10,200 plus a pig of unknown value. The farmer took away $6825 because Natalie only worked 5 months. If Natalie worked the remaining 7 months, she would have been paid the additional $6825.

Now we can find the value of one month's work by dividing: $6825 ÷ 7 = $975

If Natalie worked a full year (12 months) for money and no pig, she would have been paid 12 x $975 = $11,700.

Because a year's work is worth $10,200 plus a pig, the pig must have a value of $11,700 - $10,200 = $1500.

Super Einstein

Answer: 3.125 square inches

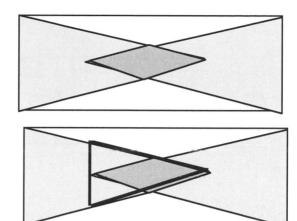

The area of each large triangle is
5 x 10 x 1/2 = 25 square inches.

The height of the triangle that is
outlined in black is 5 inches. (1/3 of 15")

The base is half the height because it is
a similar triangle to the 5 x 10 triangle.
The base is 2.5 inches

Area of the triangle outlined in black: 2.5 x 5 x 1/2 = 6.25 square inches.

The two small triangles within the triangle outlined in black have heights of 2.5 inches and
bases of 1.25 inches.
Area: 2.5 x 1.25 x 1/2 = 1.5625
Area of both small triangles: 2 x 1.5625 = 3.125

Area of overlapping part: Triangle outlined in black minus the two small triangles:
6.25 - 3.125 = 3.125

Draw a Picture

Level 1

1) Tuesday

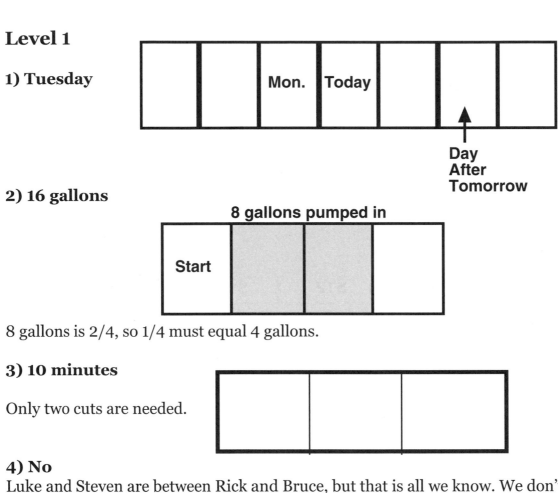

2) 16 gallons

8 gallons is 2/4, so 1/4 must equal 4 gallons.

3) 10 minutes

Only two cuts are needed.

4) No
Luke and Steven are between Rick and Bruce, but that is all we know. We don't know if Luke is taller or Steve is taller.

Rick

Luke   Steve

Bruce

5) One mile

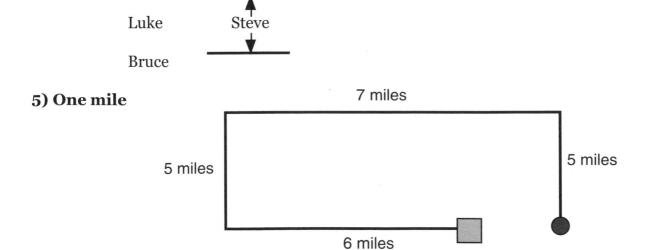

Level 2

1) 16 posts

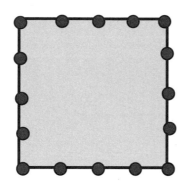

2) $192

Guitar	Charity		
	$12	$12	$12
	$12	$12	$12
	$12	$12	$12

9 boxes left that total $108. Each box is 108 ÷ 9 = $12

$12 x 4 = $48 for a quarter of the box. The entire box is 48 x 4 = $192

3) 2 miles

The sound makes a round trip from Clark to the wall and back. The round trip is 20 ÷ 5 = 4 miles, so the distance to the wall must be 2 miles.

4) 628 square feet

The area of the entire circle: 20 x 20 x 3.14 = 1256 square feet

Half circle: 1256 ÷ 2 = 628 square feet

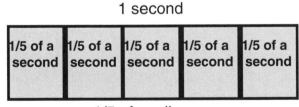

5) 1/25 of a mile

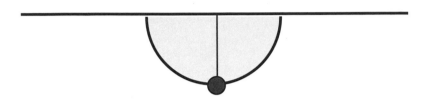

Divide the one second into 5 parts

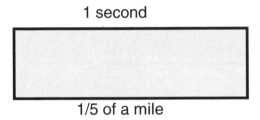

Each part must be 1/5 of 1/5 mile or 1/25 of a mile

Level 3

1) $10\frac{2}{3}$ **gallons**

4 gallons make up 3/8 of the tank,

so 1/8 tank must equal $4 \div 3 = 1\frac{1}{3}$ gallons

There are 8/8 in a tank so $8 \times 1\frac{1}{3} = 10\frac{2}{3}$

4 gallons

Gas in tank at start

2) Friday

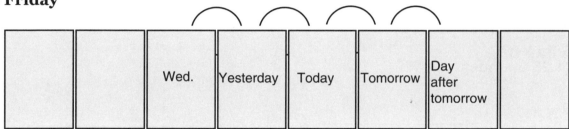

Move back four days from the day after tomorrow. Yesterday must be Thursday.
14 days before Thursday is also a Thursday, so 13 days must be a Friday.

3) 6 rockets

X................X..................X..................X..................X..................X
 12 minutes   12 minutes   12 minutes   12 minutes   12 minutes

(The first rocket does not blast off after 12 minutes, it begins the sequence.)

4) 193.5 Square feet

Area of yard: 30 x 30 = 900 square feet
        Area of watered part: 15 x 15 x 3.14 = 706.50 square feet
            Unwatered area (Subtract) : 900 - 706.50 = 193.50

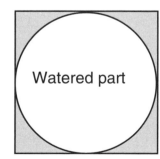

Watered part

5) 7 inches

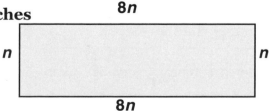

8n

n   n

8n

Perimeter: n + n + 8n + 8n = 126
            18n = 126
            n = 7

Einstein

1) 60 pounds

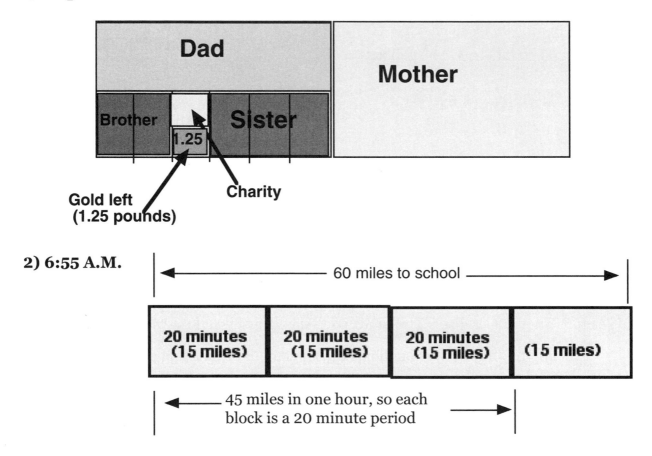

2) 6:55 A.M.

The total amount of time Warren took was 1 hour and 20 minutes because each block is a 20 minute span of time.

Warren arrived at 8:15 minus 1 hour and 20 minutes = 6:55

3) $35,000
Claudia: 1/5 or 4/20
Karen: 1/2 or 10/20
Kath: 1/4 or 5/20
20 is the common denominator, so divide a rectangle into 20 pieces.

Claudia	Claudia	Kath	Kath	Kath	Karen	Karen	Karen	Karen	Karen
Claudia	Claudia	**Sara $1750**	Kath	Kath	Karen	Karen	Karen	Karen	Karen

Sara is 1/20 , so 1/20 is equal to $1750. 20 parts x $1750 = $35,000

4) 288 gallons

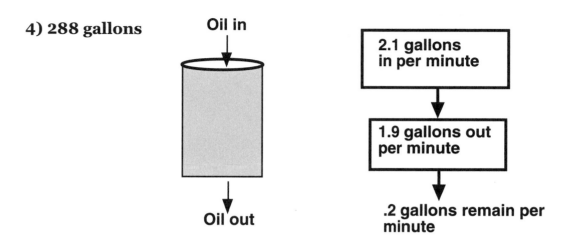

.2 or 1/5 gallon per minute
24 hours is equal to 24 x 60 = 1440 minutes.
1/5 gallon per minute x 1440 minutes = 288 gallons

5) 2198 square feet

The area of top: 10 x 10 x 3.14 = 314 square feet
Bottom: Resting on the ground

The area of the round part can be found
by cutting along the dotted line and flattening
the cylinder into a rectangle.

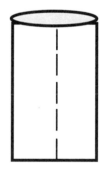

The length of the rectangle is the circumference
of the circle: 20 x 3.14 = 62.8 feet

Width of the rectangle is the height of the cylinder: 30 feet

Area of the round part (which is a rectangle) 62.8 x 30 = 1884 square feet.

1884 square feet + 314 square feet = 2198 square feet.

Super Einstein

Answer: 4 feet

Each odd fold makes a rectangle whose length is twice its width.

13th fold:

Area: n x 2n = 9/32

$2n^2 = 9/32$

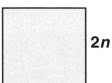

Divide both sides by 2: $n^2 = 9/64$

Square root each side: n = 3/8

12th fold: 2n and 2n

11th fold: 2n and 4n
10th fold: 4n and 4n
9th fold: 4n and 8n
8th fold: 8n and 8n
7th fold: 8n and 16n
6th fold: 16n and 16n
5th fold: 16n and 32n
4th fold: 32n and 32n
3rd fold: 32n and 64n
2nd fold: 64n and 64n
1st fold: 64n and 128n
Original: 128n and 128n

n is equal to 3/8 :   128n = 128 x 3/8 = 48 inches

Venn Diagrams

Level 1

1)   **Things that are red**

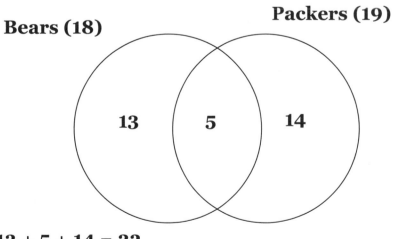

Fruits

Banana

Cardinal

Apple
Strawberry

Stop Sign

Orange

2) The pets that they both have: cat, dog

3) 32

Bears (18)   Packers (19)

13   5   14

13 + 5 + 14 = 32

4) 21

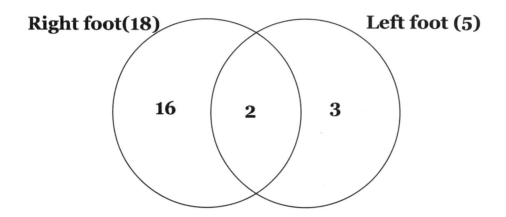

5) 25 children

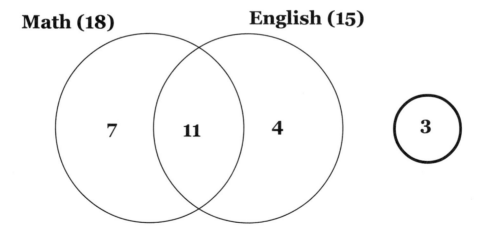

7 + 11 + 4 + 3 = 25

Level 2

1) 6 children

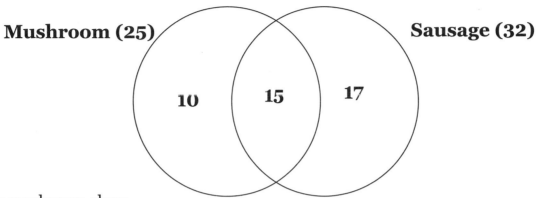

Mushroom (25)   **Sausage (32)**

10 like mushroom alone
17 like sausage alone
15 like both

_____

42 children-----Because there are 48 children in the classroom, then there must be 6 who like neither topping.

2) 34 dogs

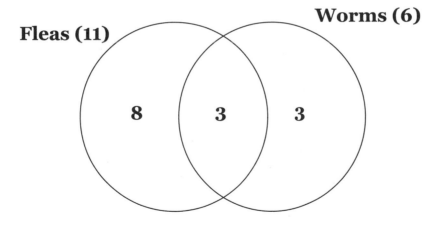

Fleas (11)   **Worms (6)**

3 dogs have fleas and worms
8 dogs have only fleas
3 dogs have only worms
_____

14 dogs

48 total - 14 dogs with some kind of parasite = 34 dogs are free of worms and fleas.

3) 13 people

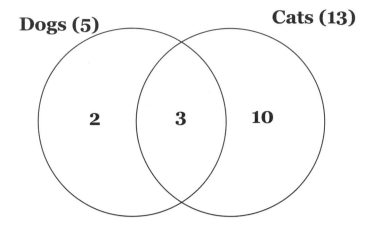

Dogs (5)   **Cats (13)**

2   3   10

The Venn Diagram adds up to 15.
28 people answered the questionnaire, so
13 must have neither pet.

4) Rat, fish. All three children have a rat and a fish as a pet.

5) Pig

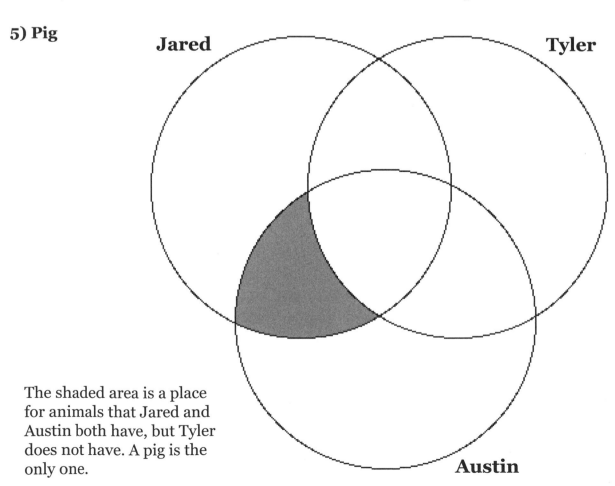

Jared   **Tyler**

Austin

The shaded area is a place
for animals that Jared and
Austin both have, but Tyler
does not have. A pig is the
only one.

Level 3

1) Square. The only rectangles that are rhombuses are squares. A rhombus is a parallelogram with 4 equal sides. The only rhombuses that are rectangles are squares.

2) **A = Scalene triangles**
B = Equilateral triangles
C = Isosceles triangles

All equilateral triangles are isosceles triangles. Scalene triangles have 3 unequal sides so they are neither isosceles nor equilateral triangles.

3) 3, 5, 7, 11, 13, 17, 19

These seven numbers are the only numbers that belong to each of the three circles. (Remember that 1 is not a prime number.)

4)

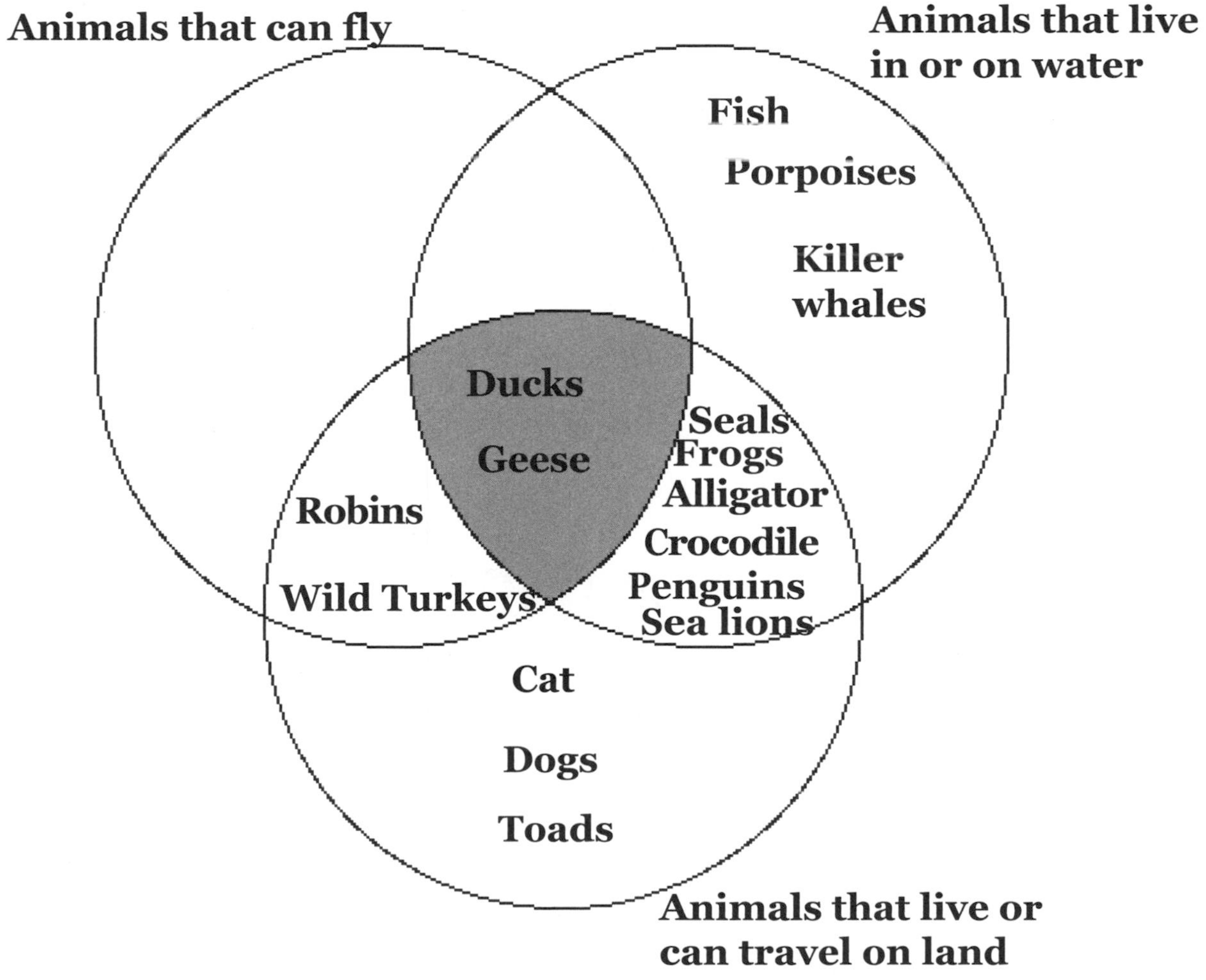

5)

Bad Location (42)

Poor customer service (13)

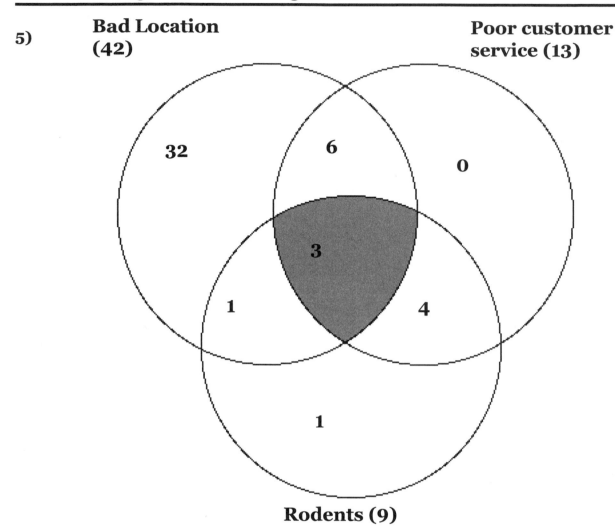

Rodents (9)

Einstein Level

1) 35 dogs

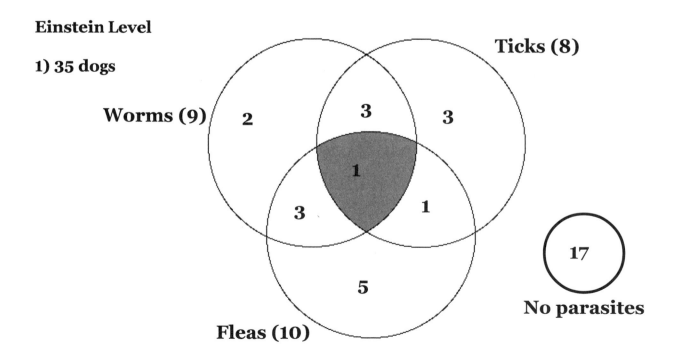

Worms (9) **Ticks (8)**

Fleas (10) **No parasites**

2) 10 students

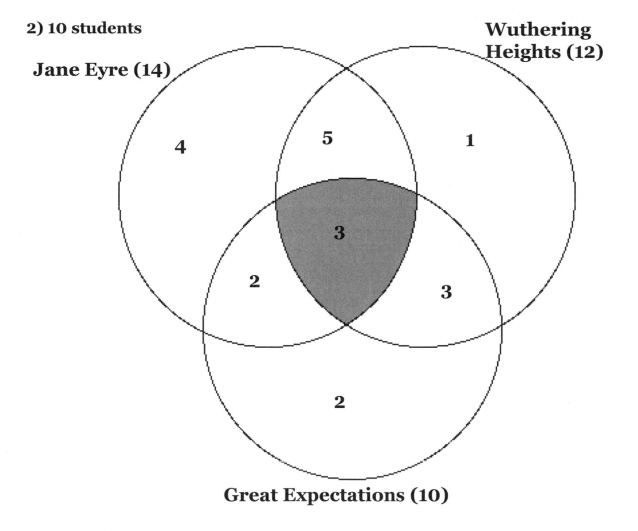

4 + 5 + 2 + 3 + 3 + 2 + 1 = 20

30 (total students) - 20 (that read something) = 10 students read none of the books

3) 30 Children

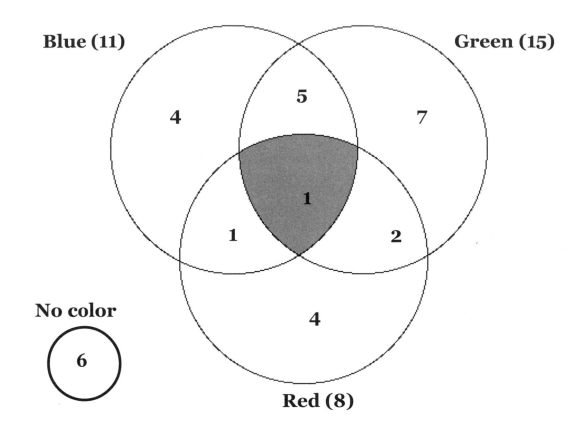

Add up all the numbers: 4 + 5 + 1 + 1 + 7 + 2 + 4 + 6 = 30

4) 8 students

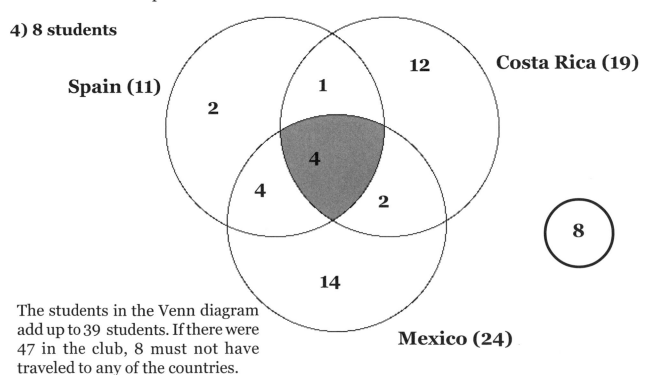

The students in the Venn diagram add up to 39 students. If there were 47 in the club, 8 must not have traveled to any of the countries.

5) 16 children had all three diseases

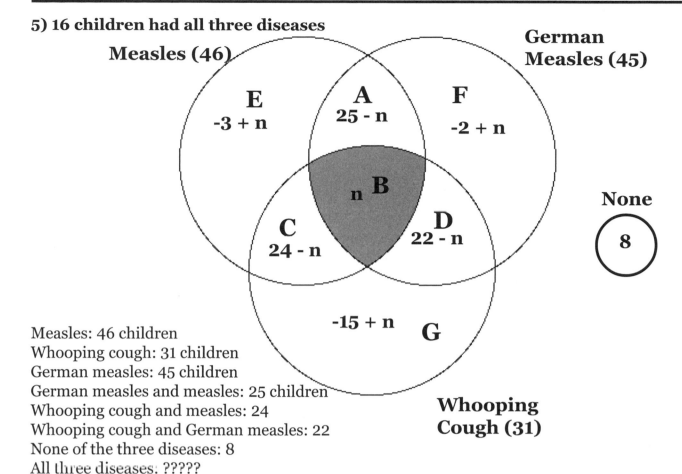

Measles: 46 children
Whooping cough: 31 children
German measles: 45 children
German measles and measles: 25 children
Whooping cough and measles: 24
Whooping cough and German measles: 22
None of the three diseases: 8
All three diseases: ?????

Because German measles and measles=25 children, section A is equal to 25-n
Because whooping cough and measles=24 children, section C is equal to 24-n
Because whooping cough and German measles=22 children, section D is equal to 22-n

Now we know that A + B + C = (25 - n) + (n) +(24 - n) which is equal to 49 -n
E is found by subtracting (49 - n) from 46: 46 - (49 - n) = **-3 + n**

We also know that C + B + D = (24 - n) + (n) + (22 - n) which is equal to 46 - n
G is found by subtracting (46 - n) from 31:   31 - (46 - n) = **-15 + n**

We also know that A + B + D = (25 - n) + (n) + (22 - n) which is equal to 47 - n
F is found by subtracting (47 - n) from 45:   45 - (47 - n) = **-2 + n**

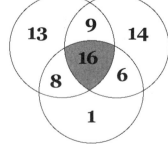

All the spaces add up to 75:
(-3 + n) + (25 - n) + (n) + (24 - n) + (- 2 + n) +(22 - n) +(- 15 + n) + (8) (no disease) = 75
Collecting: n + 59 = 75   n = 16

Super Einstein Level

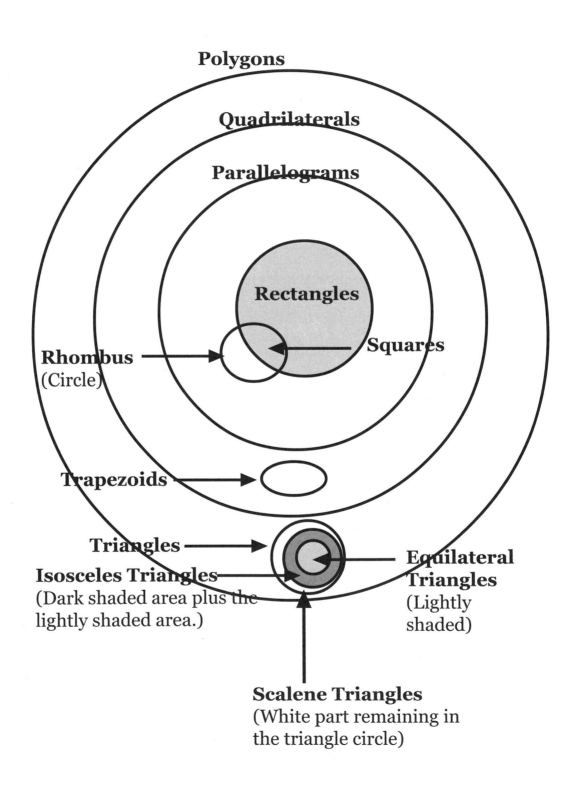

Language of Algebra

Level 1

1) 10n

meters: n
decimeters: 10n

There are 10 decimeters in each meter. To change meters to decimeters simply multiply by 10. n meters x 10 = 10n decimeters

2) 8n

gallons: n
pints: 8n

There are 2 pints in each quart, so there are 4 x 2 = 8 pints in each gallon.

3) 24n

There are 24 hours in each of the n days.

4) 12n

There are 12 inches in each of the n feet.

5)   Rachel's age: 3n
         Luke's age: 9n

Rachel's age is three times Dan's age or 3 x n = 3n
Luke's age is three times Rachel's age or 3 x 3n = 9n

6) 3n

There are 3 feet in a yard.

7) 5n

If there are 6 nickels, the value is 6 x 5 = 30 cents
If there are 8 nickels, the value is 8 x 5 = 40 cents
If there are n nickels, the value is n x 5 = 5n

8) 50*n*

William travels 50 miles each hour. If he travels 4 hours, he will go 50 x 4 = 200 miles.

If he travels n hours, he will go a distance of 50 x n = 50n miles.

9) *n*π

Multiply the diameter by pi. n x π = nπ

10) *n* + 4

Largest: n + 4
next: n + 3
next: n + 2
next: n + 1
Smallest: n

Level 2

1) *n*/10

To change decimeters to meters, divide by 10.
If you had 80 decimeters, you would have 80 ÷ 10 = 8 meters
If you had n decimeters, you would have n ÷ 10 = n/10 meters

2) 1,000,000*n*
There are 1,000,000 millimeters in each kilometer.

3) 4*n* + 30
Each number is 5 larger

Largest: n + 15
Next: n + 10
Next: n + 5
Smallest: n

(n) + (n + 5) + (n + 10) + (n + 15) = 4n + 30

4) 9*n* + 55

Nolan's bonus is $55.
Nolan's hourly pay is $9 x n hours: = 9n
Total pay: 9n + 55

5) *n/2*

If Amelda had 10 shoes, she would have 10 ÷ 2 = 5 pairs of shoes
If Amelda had n shoes, she would have n ÷ 2 = n/2 pairs of shoes

6) .85*n*

15% of n is .15n   That is the amount that is subtracted from n
                                       n - .15n = .85n

7) .25*n*

Each quarter is worth .25 dollars. n quarters are worth .25 x n = .25n

8) $\frac{1}{3}n + 6000$

1/3 of Claudia's salary is $\frac{1}{3}n$ $6000 more than Claudia's salary is $\frac{1}{3}n$ + 6000

9) 1550 - *n*

The total cost is 1550. Take away the cost of the chair (n) and the remaining is the cost of the desk.

10) 180 - *n*

Because the number of degrees in a straight line is equal to 180°, the total of both angles is 180°. The measurement of angle #2 is therefore 180° - n.

Level 3

1) *n*/3600

There are 60 seconds x 60 minutes = 3600 seconds in an hour.

If Joe talked for 10,000 seconds, he would have talked for
10,000 ÷ 3600 = 2.78 hours

Joe talked for *n* seconds: *n* ÷ 3600 = *n*/3600 hours

2) 85n

Number of dimes: n   Value of the dimes: 10 cents x n = 10n
Number of quarters: 3n   Value of the quarters: 25 cents x 3n = 75n

Value of the coins in the box: 10n + 75n = 85n

3) 360 - 5.5n

There are 360 degrees in a quadrilateral.
The three given angles have a total measure of 2.5n + 2n + n = 5.5n
The remaining angle must equal 360 - 5.5n

4) .000001n

A millimeter is 1/1000 of a meter.
A meter is 1/1000 of a kilometer.
Therefore, a millimeter must be 1/1,000,000 of a kilometer.

5) n/8 or 1/8 of n

There are 8 pints in a gallon, so there is 1/8 of a gallon in each pint.
If you had 24 pints, you would have 24 ÷ 8 = 3 gallons.
If you had 16 pints, you would have 16 ÷ 8 = 2 gallons.

If you had n pints, you would have n ÷ 8 = $\dfrac{n}{8}$ gallons.

6) 7n

Because a circle has 360 degrees, 45° is 1/8 of the circumference and is called n.
The remaining section of the circumference is 7/8 of the circle, which would be equal to 7n.

7) 1.06n

Guitar: n dollars
Tax: 6% of n is equal to .06 x n = .06n
Total: n + .06n = 1.06n

8) 19n

Draw a picture. The perimeter can be
found by adding each side.
n + n + 8.5n + 8.5n = 19n

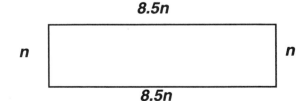

9) 1000 - 5*n*

Number of 5-cent stamps: n
Value of 5-cent stamps: 5 x n = 5n

Number of 10-cent stamps: 100 - n
Because the total number of stamps is 100 and there are n 5-cent stamps, there must be (100 - n) 10-cent stamps.
Value of 10-cent stamps: 10 cents each stamp x (100 - n) = 1000 - 10n

Value of all stamps: (5n) + (1000-10n) = 1000 - 5n

10) 8*n* + 3

Number of cows: n
Number of cow legs: 4 x n = 4n (Number of cows is n and four legs per cow)

Number of chickens: 2 x n = 2n (Twice as many chickens as cows)
Number of chicken legs: 4n (Number of chickens is 2n and two legs per chicken)
Tripod's legs: 3
4n + 4n + 3 = 8n + 3

Einstein Level

1) 5*n* miles

Distance Luke drove: 55n (55 miles each hour and n hours: 55 x n = 55n)
Distance mom drove: 60n (60 miles each hour and n hours: 60 x n = 60n)
60n - 55n = 5n

2) 320 - 4*n*

Number of ducks: n   Number of duck legs: Two legs each x n ducks = 2n
Number of horses: 80 - n   (A total of 80 animals and n ducks. Therefore there
                            are 80 - n horses.)
Number of horse legs: 4(80 - n) = 320 - 4n

{A total of (80 - n) horses x 4 legs for each horse = 4(80 - n) = 320 - 4n}

3) 50*n*

Speed: 72 miles per hour
Distance: n miles
Distance = Speed x Time   so   Time = Distance ÷ Speed
Time: n miles ÷ 72 mph = n/72   hours

If you traveled 1000 miles at 72 mph, your time would be 1000 ÷ 72 = 13.89 hours.
If you traveled n miles at 72 mph, your time would be n ÷ 72 = n/72 hours.

Because there are 3600 seconds in each hour, we can change n/72 hours to seconds by multiplying by 3600. n/72 x 3600 = 3600n/72 = 50n

4) 64*n* dollars

Width: n
Length: 3n
Perimeter: n + n + 3n + 3n = 8n
Cost of fencing: 8n x $8 = 64n dollars

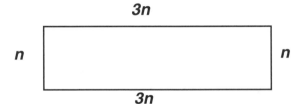

5) .864*n*

Regular price of the guitar: n
Discount: 20% of n or .2n
Discounted price: n - .2n = .8n   (Regular price of n minus the discount of .2n)
Tax: 8% of the price or .08 x .8n = .064n
Total cost: Price of .8n + tax of .064n = .864n

6) 360 - 2*n*

All four angles add up to 360°.
The measure of the angle across from n is also n, so 360 - n - n = The measure of the remaining two angles A and B.

7) 2*n* + 402

Cows: n
Cow legs: 4n (Number of cows x 4 legs per cow)
Ducks: 200 - n (200 animals minus the number of cows)
Duck legs: 2(200 - n) = 400 - 2n (Number of ducks x 2 legs per duck)
Farmer's legs: 2

Add the legs: 4n + 400 - 2n + 2 = 2n + 402

8) $n + 3$

Largest number: n + 6
Next: n + 5
Next: n + 4
Next: n + 3
Next: n + 2
Next: n + 1
Smallest number: n

The average is found by adding all seven numbers and dividing by seven.

$$\frac{n + (n+1) + (n+2) + (n+3) + (n+4) + (n+5) + (n+6)}{7}$$

9) $.729n$

Value new: n
Value after 1 year: 90% of n   or   .9 x n = .9n
Value after 2 years: 90% of .9n   or   .9 x .9n = .81n
Value after 3 years: 90% of .81n   or   .9 x .81n = .729n

10) $.215n^2$

Area of the square: n x n = n^2
Radius: .5n

Area of the circle: π x .5n x .5n = 3.14 x .25n^2 = .785n^2

Area of shaded part: Area of square minus area of circle

$$n^2 - .785 = .215n^2$$

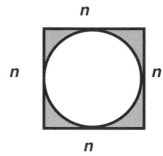

Super Einstein

Answer: $.6818n$ miles per hour

Gradually turn feet per second into miles per hour.

Step 1: You first must change the speed to feet per hour.

Step 2: Because there are 3600 seconds in an hour, multiply the feet per second by 3600 to find feet per hour. n feet per second x 3600 = 3600n feet per hour.

Step 3: To change feet to miles, simply divide by 5280. (There are 5280 feet in each mile.) 3600n feet ÷ 5280 = .6818n miles per hour

Solving Equations

Level 1

1) $n = 8$

$$2n + 8 = 24$$
Subtract: $-8 \quad -8$

$$2n = 16 \qquad n = 8$$

2) $n = 18$

$$5n - 5 = 85$$
Add: $+5 \quad +5$

$$5n = 90 \qquad n = 18$$

3) $n = 12$

$$2n + 8 - n = 20$$
Collect: $n + 8 = 20$
Subtract: $-8 \quad -8$

$$n = 12$$

4) $n = 8$

$$7n + 4 + n - 5 = 63$$
Collect: $8n - 1 = 63$
Add: $+1 \quad +1$

$$8n = 64$$
Divide by 8: $n = 8$

5) $n = 9$

$$2n + 1 = n + 10$$
n's on one side: $-n \qquad -n$

$$n + 1 = 10$$
Subtract: $-1 \quad -1$
$$n = 9$$

6) $n = 3.5$

$$2n - 7 = 0$$

Add: $+7 \quad +7$

$$2n = 7$$

Divide by 2: $n = 3.5$

7) $n = 2$

$$n + 2n + 3n + 4n = 2 + 3 + 4 + 5 + 6$$

Collect: $10n = 20$
Divide by 10: $n = 2$

8) $n = -5$

$$\frac{1}{2}n + 1\frac{1}{2}n = -10$$

Collect: $2n = -10$
                $n = -5$

9) $n = 3$

$$4n - 8 = n + 1$$

n's on one side: $-n \qquad -n$
                    $3n - 8 = 1$
Add: $+8 \quad +8$
                    $3n = 9$

Divide by 3: $n = 3$

10) $n = 1$

$$100n = 100$$

Divide by 100: $n = 1$

Level 2

1) $n = 10$

$$n - n = 10 - n$$

Collect: $0 = 10 - n$

Subtract 10: $-10 \quad -10$

         $-10 = -n$ Multiply both sides by -1 $n = 10$

2) $n = 118$

$$2n - 1\tfrac{1}{2}n = 59$$

Collect: $\tfrac{1}{2}n = 59$

Want one n so multiply by 2: $\tfrac{1}{2}n \times 2 = 59 \times 2$

$$n = 118$$

3) $n = 5$

$$2n + 10 = 3n + 5$$

n's on one side: $-2n \qquad -2n$

                $10 = n + 5$

Subtract 5: $-5 \qquad -5$

                $5 = n$

4) $n = 0$

$$2n = 4n$$

n's on one side: $-2n \quad -2n$

             $0 = 2n$ $n = 0$

5) $n = 2$

$$n + 9n - 8 - 5 = 2n + 3$$

Collect: $10n - 13 = 2n + 3$

n's on one side: $-2n \qquad -2n$

               $8n - 13 = 3$

Add: $+13 \quad +13$

               $8n = 16$

Divide by 8: $n = 2$

6) $n = 1000$

$$\frac{1}{10}n = 100$$

Want one n so multiply both sides by 10: $10 \times \frac{1}{10}n = 10 \times 100$

$$n = 1000$$

7) $n = 8$

$$n^2 = 64$$

Just one n so take square root of both sides: Square root of n^2 = Square root of 64

$$n = 8$$

8) $n = 9$

$$n + 9n - 90 = 0$$

Collect: $10n - 90 = 0$

Add 90: $+90 \quad +90$

$$10n = 90$$

Divide both sides by 10: $n = 9$

9) $n = 5$

$$n^2 + 9 = 34$$

n^2 needs to be alone so subtract 9 from both sides: $-9 \quad -9$

$$n^2 = 25$$

Just one n so take square root of both sides: $n = 5$

10) $n = 1$

$$10n - 9n + 8n - 7n + 6n = 10 - 9 + 8 - 7 + 6$$

Collect: $8n = 8$

Just one n so divide each side by 8: $8n \div 8 = 8 \div 8$

$$n = 1$$

Level 3

1) $n = 50$

$$- n = -50$$

Multiply each side by -1: $n = 50$

2) $n = -640$

$$-\frac{1}{8}n = 80$$

Want one n so we will multiply both sides by 8: $8 \times -\frac{1}{8}n = 8 \times 80$

$$-n = 640$$
Multiply by -1: $n = -640$

3) $n = 1/2$ or $-1/2$

$$n^2 = \frac{1}{4}$$

Want n so take square root of both sides: $n = 1/2$ $(\frac{1}{2} x \frac{1}{2} = \frac{1}{4})$

4) $n = 1/4$

$$n = 3n - \frac{1}{2}$$

n's on one side: $-n$ $-n$

$$0 = 2n - \frac{1}{2}$$

Add 1/2 to both side: $+\frac{1}{2}$ $+\frac{1}{2}$

$$\frac{1}{2} = 2n$$

Want one n so we will divide by 2: $1/4 = n$

5) $n = .05$

$$10n = .5$$
Want one n so we will divide both sides by 10: $n = .05$

6) $n = -1$

	$-5n - 5n - 5 = 5$
Collect:	-10n -5 = 5
Add 5 to both sides:	+5 +5
	-10n = 10

Want one n so divide both sides by -10:   n = -1

7) $n = 121$

$$\frac{1}{11}n = 11$$

Want one n so multiply both sides by 11: n = 121

8) $n = 5/3$

$$\frac{3}{5}n = 1$$

Want one n so multiply both sides by 5/3: n = 5/3

9) $n = 1$

	$1 - n = n - 1$
n's on one side:	+n +n
	1 = 2n - 1
Add 1 to both sides:	+1 +1
	2 = 2n

Divide both sides by 2:   1 = n

10) $n = 5/2$ or $-5/2$

$$n^2 = 6\frac{1}{4}$$

Want one n so take square root of both sides: square root of n^2 = square root of 25/4

$$n = 5/2$$

Einstein Level

1) $n = 1/10$ or $-1/10$

$$n^2 - 1 = \frac{-99}{100}$$

Add 1 to both sides: $+1 \quad +1$

$$n^2 = 1/100$$

Square root of both sides: $n = 1/10$ or $-1/10$

2) $n = 0$

                           $-n = n$

n's all on one side: $+n \quad +n$

                           $0 = 2n \qquad n = 0$

3) $n = 85$

$$n + .07n = \$90.95$$

Collect: $1.07n = \$90.95$

Want only one n so divide both sides by 1.07: $n = 85$

4) $n = 8$ or -8

$$\frac{1}{n^2} = \frac{3}{192}$$

Cross-multiply: $3n^2 = 192$

Divide both sides by 3: $n^2 = 64$

Square root of both sides: $n = 8$ or -8

5) $n = 10,000$

$$n + \frac{1}{2}n + \frac{1}{4}n + \frac{1}{8}n + \frac{1}{16}n = 19,375$$

Collect: $1\frac{15}{16}n = 19,375$

Want only one n so divide both sides by $1\frac{15}{16}$: $n = 10,000$

6) $n = 6$

$$\frac{1}{n} + \frac{2}{n} + \frac{3}{n} = 1$$

Because the denominators are all n,

you can make one fraction:

$$\frac{1 + 2 \quad 3}{n} = 1$$

This is the same as:

$$\frac{6}{n} = 1 \quad \text{Now we know that n must equal 6}$$

7) $n = 7$

$$5^{n-1} = 15{,}625$$

What power of 5 is equal to 15,625? The answer is 5 x 5 x 5 x 5 x 5 x 5 or n^6

Equation: n-1 = 6   n = 7

8) $n = 6$

$$2^n = 4^{n-3}$$

We must change the 4 to a 2 to make
the exponents easy to work with.

$$2^n = (2^2)^{n-3}$$

$(2^2)^{n-3}$ is equal to $2^{2(n-3)}$

New equation: $2^n = 2^{2(n-3)}$
Final equation: n = 2(n-3)   n = 2n - 6   n = 6

9) $n = 10$

$$\frac{1}{n} + \frac{2}{n} + \frac{3}{n} + \frac{4}{n} = 1$$

This is equal to $\dfrac{10}{n} = 1$ n must equal 10

10) $n = 2.5$

$$\frac{1}{n} + \frac{3}{5} = 1$$

Common denominator is 5n: $\dfrac{5}{5n} + \dfrac{3n}{5n} = 1$ same as: $\dfrac{5 + 3n}{5n} = 1$

Cross-multiply: 5 + 3n = 5n
n's on one side: 5 = 2n   n = 2.5

Super Einstein

Answer: n = 15

Solve for n: $\dfrac{31}{170} = \dfrac{1}{5\dfrac{1}{2\dfrac{1}{n}}}$ $\dfrac{31}{170} = \dfrac{1}{5\dfrac{1}{\boxed{2\dfrac{1}{n}}}}$ ⟶ Is equal to $\dfrac{2n+1}{n}$

$\dfrac{31}{170} = \dfrac{1}{5\dfrac{1}{\boxed{\dfrac{2n+1}{n}}}}$ ⟶ Is equal to $\dfrac{n}{2n+1}$

$\dfrac{31}{170} = \dfrac{1}{\boxed{5\dfrac{n}{2n+1}}}$ ⟶ Is equal to $\dfrac{5(2n+1)\;n}{2n+1} = \dfrac{11n+5}{2n+1}$

$\dfrac{31}{170} = \dfrac{1}{\dfrac{11n+5}{2n+1}}$ $\dfrac{31}{170} = \dfrac{1}{\boxed{\dfrac{11n+5}{2n+1}}}$ ⟶ Is equal to $\dfrac{2n+1}{11n+5}$

$\dfrac{31}{170} = \dfrac{2n+1}{11n+5}$ Cross-multiply 341n + 155 = 340n + 170

n's on one side so subtract 340n from both sides: n + 155 = 170

Subtract 155 from both sides: n = 15

Solving Algebra Problems

Level 1

1) 65 pounds

Dog: n
Laura: n + 45
Equation: 2n + 45 = 85
              Subtract 45 from both sides: 2n = 40
                 Divide both sides by 2: n = 20

2) 85 cents

Ruler: n
Yardstick: n + 45
Equation: 2n + 45 = 125
              Subtract 45 from both sides: 2n = 80
                 Divide both sides by 2: n = 40

3) 21 years old

Joel: n
Jane: 2n
Equation: n + 2n = 63   3n = 63
              Divide both sides by 3: n = 21

4) $30

Cheap backpack: n
Expensive backpack: n + 15
Equation: 2n + 15 = 75
              Subtract 15 from both sides: 2n = 60
                 Divide both sides by 2: n = 30

5) 112

Smaller number: n
Larger number: n + 2
Equation: 2n + 2 = 226
              Subtract 2 from both sides: 2n = 224
                 Divide both sides by 2: n = 112

Level 2

1) 5 pounds
Hamster: n
Cat: n + 10
Dog: n + 10
Equation: 3n + 20 = 35 (Add all three pets)
Subtract 20 from both sides: 3n = 15
Divide both sides by 3: n = 5

2) 31 hours
Hours worked: n
Hourly pay: 7.5 x n hours worked = 7.5n
Bonus: $80
Equation: 7.5n + 80 = 312.50
Subtract 80 from both sides: 7.5n = 232.50
Divide both sides by 7.5: n = 31

3) 7 miles
1st day: n
2nd day: n +1
3rd day: n + 2
4th day: n + 3
5th day: n + 4
6th day: n + 5
7th day: n + 6
Equation: 7n + 21 = 70 miles
Subtract 21 from both sides: 7n = 49
Divide both sides by 7: n = 7

4) Dan is in debt $18
Dan's debt: n
Luke's debt: 3n
Equation: 4n = 72
Divide both sides by 4: n = 18

5) 15 nickels
Number of nickels: n
Number of dimes: n
Value of the nickels: 5 x n = 5n
Value of the dimes: 10 x n = 10n
Equation: 5n + 10n = 225   15n = 225
Divide both sides by 15: n = 15

Level 3

1) $\dfrac{1}{16}$n

Start: n   Monday: $\dfrac{1}{2}$n   Tuesday: $\dfrac{1}{2}$ of $\dfrac{1}{2}$n = $\dfrac{1}{4}$n

Wednesday: $\dfrac{1}{2}$ of $\dfrac{1}{4}$n = $\dfrac{1}{8}$n   Thursday: $\dfrac{1}{2}$ of $\dfrac{1}{8}$n = $\dfrac{1}{16}$n

2) 352 feet

Ranger's height: n
Tree's height: 64n
Smaller tree's height: 64n - 112
Equation: n + 64n + (64n - 112) = 597.5   (Add the heights of all three.)
          Collect: 129n - 112 = 597.5
                    Add 112 to both sides: 129n = 709.5
                              Divide both sides by 129: n = 5.5

Ranger is 5.5 feet. The tree is 64 times the height of the ranger: 64 x 5.5 = 352

3) 17 inches

Equation: 1.2n + n + .5n + .5n = 54.4
          Collect: 3.2n = 54.4
                    Divide both sides by 3.2: n = 17

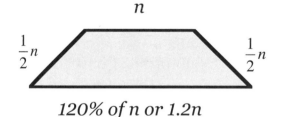

120% of n or 1.2n

4) $480
Computer: n
Tax: .07 x n or .07n
Equation: The sales tax = $33.60   .07n = $33.60
                    Divide both sides by .07: n = 480

5) 31 ducks
Number of ducks: n   Duck legs: 2 x n = 2n
Number of cows: 2n   Cow legs: 4 x 2n = 8n
                                    Tripod's legs: 3
Equation: 2n + 8n + 3 = 313
          Collect: 10n + 3 = 313
                    Subtract 3 from each side: 10n = 310
                              Divide each side by 10: n = 31

Einstein Level

1) 24 years old

Language of algebra in 1980

Michael: n
Nancy: 2n
Ric: 4n

Language of algebra in 1992

Michael: n + 12
Nancy: 2n + 12
Ric: 4n + 12

Equation: (n + 12) + (2n + 12) + (4n + 12) = 78
     Collect: 7n + 36 = 78
          Subtract 36 from each side: 7n = 42
               Divide both sides by 7: n = 6

2) 16

Language of algebra

Number of 37-cent stamps: n
Number of 3-cent stamps: 3n
Number of 5-cent stamps: .5n

Value of 37-cent stamps: n x 37 = 37n
Value of 3-cent stamps: 3n x 3 = 9n
Value of 5-cent stamps: .5n x 5 = 2.5n
Value of coins: 52 cents

Equation: 37n + 9n + 2.5n + 52 = 828
     Collect: 48.5n + 52 = 828
          Subtract 52 from each side: 48.5n = 776
               Divide both sides by 48.5: n = 16

3) 12 inches by 12 inches

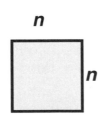

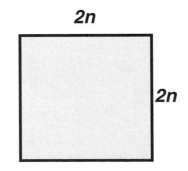

The area of the small square is n x n = n^2

The area of the larger square is 2n x 2n = $4n^2$

If the larger square is 432 square inches larger than the smaller square, then

$4n^2 - n^2 = 432$

Subtract: $4n^2 - n^2 = 3n^2$

      New equation: $3n^2 = 432$

          Divide both sides by 3: $n^2 = 144$

What number multiplied by itself equals 144? The answer of course is 12.

4) More than 400 minutes

Language of algebra

Minutes per month that Rachel talks: n
Current phone company cost: 12 cents x n = 12n
Discount phone company cost: .5 cent x n = .5n + 4600 cents ($46 monthly fee)

When are the charges equal?
Equation: 12n = .5n + 4600
    Subtract .5n from both sides: 11.5n = 4600
        Divide both sides by 11.5:   n = 400

When Rachel talks 400 minutes per month, both companies will charge the same. If she talks more than 400 minutes, the discount company is the better deal.

5) 16 nickels

Language of algebra

Number of nickels: n   Value of nickels: 5 x n = 5n
Number of dimes: 2.5n   Value of dimes: 10 x 2.5n = 25n
Number of quarters: 5n   Value of quarters: 25 x 5n = 125n

Equation: 5n + 25n + 125n = 2480
    Collect: 155n = 2480
        Divide both sides by 155: n = 16

Super Einstein

Answer: 284 feet of fencing

Language of algebra
Feet of fencing : n
Perimeter of square garden: n

Square garden's area = $\frac{1}{4}n \times \frac{1}{4}n = \frac{n^2}{16}$

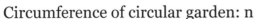

Circumference of circular garden: n
We need to find the area of a circle with a circumference of n.

Circumference = π x diameter
n = π x diameter
Divide both sides by π: diameter = n/π

Radius: $\frac{n}{\pi} \div 2 = \frac{n}{2\pi}$

Area = pi x radius x radius

Area = $\pi \times \frac{n}{2\pi} \times \frac{n}{2\pi}$ Area = $\frac{\pi n^2}{4\pi^2}$

Reduce by canceling pi: $\frac{n^2}{4\pi}$ or $\frac{n^2}{4 \times 3.14}$ or $\frac{n^2}{12.56}$ (area of circle)

The problem says that the difference between the square's area and the circle's area is equal to 1380 square feet.

Equation: $\frac{n^2}{12.56}$ (area of circle) - $\frac{n^2}{16}$ (area of square) = 1380

Common denominator is 200.96

$\frac{16n^2 - 12.56n^2}{200.96} = 1380$ Subtract numerator: $\frac{3.44n^2}{200.96} = 1380$

Cross-multiply: $3.44n^2 = 277,324.8$

Divide both sides by 3.44: $n^2 = 80,617.7$ n = 283.9

Logic

Level 1

1) No

All dogs are mammals, but not all mammals are dogs.
All squares are rectangles, but all rectangles are not squares.

2) No

If Susan is riding her bike, then we know she must be wearing a helmet. She may also wear her helmet when she sleds or skateboards.

3) True

This is similar to the following statement: All collies are dogs and all dogs are mammals, therefore all collies arc mammals. Of course this is true.

4) 9

Dale could pick 5 similar quarters in a row, but the most he could pick and still not have 5 quarters from the same country is 4 American and 4 Canadian. His next pick would guarantee 5 like quarters.

5) 1st drawing

The set of all rectangles is larger than the set of all squares. The set of all squares is inside the set of all rectangles.

Level 2

1) No

Dan could have failed the test for a variety of other reasons: Being sick, cheating, marking the wrong bubbles. All we know is that if Dan decides not to study, he is guaranteed to not pass the test. If he studies he has a chance of passing the test, but it isn't a sure thing.

2) No

It could have been sunny and a friend threw a water balloon.

3) 2nd drawing

The set of times I got wet is the larger set. It includes things such as a water balloon attack, water from a squirt gun, a car driving by and splashing, and rain.

4) Faulty logic

There are hundreds of times more minivans on the road than Corvettes, so there will be more deaths involving minivans, even if they are the most safely driven cars on the road.

5) More accidents occur within 30 miles of one's home because that is where the majority of travel takes place.

Level 3

1) 1:4:1

Original cup	Spilled cup	Refilled cup

Blue
Green
Red

Empty
Blue
Green
Red

Green
Blue
Green
Red

2) No
All squares have diagonals that bisect each corner angle, but rhombuses also have diagonals that cut the corner angles into two equal angles.

3) No
There could be many left-handed players who do not pick goalie as their favorite position.

Everything inside the large circle: All players on the soccer team
The small dark circle: Players who picked goalie as their favorite position
The lightly shaded part within the large circle: Right-handed players
Everything inside the white circle including the dark circle: Left-handed players

4)

> **Step 1**: Fill the 3-quart container and pour it into the 5-quart container.
> **Step 2**: Fill the 3-quart container and pour as much as you can into the 5-quart. (2 quarts) This will leave one quart in the 3-quart container.
> **Step 3**: Empty the 5-quart and pour the one quart into the 5-quart.
> **Step 4**: Fill the 3-quart and pour it into the 5-quart. Now there are 4 quarts in the 5-quart container.

5) Yes

If she eats the donuts she WILL wake up in a fog.
> If she is in a fog, she WILL NOT do well on the test.
> > If she doesn't do well on the test, she WILL NOT get a scholarship.

Einstein Level

1) 2000 miles

Because the distance is 3000 miles, there will be a total of 12,000 tire miles (3000 miles x 4 tires)
12,0000 tire miles divided by 6 tires = 2000 miles each tire.

2) Guilty

The only way the rabbit would be lying is if it had something to gain from lying.
The owl said that the rabbit had nothing to gain from lying, therefore
the rabbit is telling the truth.
Because the rabbit is telling the truth, the opossum is lying.
If the raccoon was innocent, the opossum would not be lying.

Because the opossum is lying, the raccoon cannot be innocent, therefore it is guilty!!

3) **Step 1**: Fill the 7-quart and pour it into the 9-quart.

Step 2: Fill the 7-quart and pour 2 quarts into the 9-quart. The 9-quart is filled and 5 quarts are remaining in the 7-quart.

Step 3: Empty the 9-quart.

Step 4: Pour the remaining 5 quarts that are in the 7-quart into the 9-quart.

Step 5: Fill the 7-quart and pour 4 quarts into the 9-quart, which will fill it. 3 quarts are remaining in the 7-quart.

Step 6: Empty the 9-quart.

Step 7: Pour the 3 quarts that are remaining in the 7-quart into the 9-quart container.

Step 8: Fill the 7-quart and pour 6 quarts into the 9-quart. This will fill it and leave 1 quart remaining in the 7-quart container.

Step 9: Empty the 9 quart.

Step 10: Pour the 1 quart from the 7-quart into the 9-quart.

Step 11: Fill the 7-quart and pour it into the 9-quart. There are now 8 quarts in the 9-quart container.

4) 4163 pounds

500 gallons = 2000 quarts

How many groups of 1.057 quarts are there in the 2000 quarts?

2000 ÷ 1.057 = 1892.15 liters
        1892.15 liters weigh 1892.15 kilograms
                1892.15 kilograms x 2.2 = 4163 pounds

5) Ask the frog the following question: "If I were to ask the rat which bridge is the safe bridge, which one would he point to?"

If the frog is the truthteller, he would tell you that the rat would point to the dangerous bridge.

If the frog is the liar, the truthtelling rat would point out the safe bridge, but the lying frog would tell you he said the dangerous bridge.

In both situations, the dangerous bridge would be pointed to. Take the other bridge.

Note: You could also ask the rat the question and the logic would remain the same.

Super Einstein

Answer:

The missing dollar is not really missing. The cost of the meal is really $27.
The $25 plus the extra two dollar tip that was given to the waitress——$27

What we have is the cost ($27) plus the refund ($3) = $30

The $30 that was originally paid is accounted for as follows:

Restaurant + regular waitress tip: $25
Three people: $3 (refund)
Waitress: $2 (extra tip)
$25 + $3 + $2 = $30

Power of Ratios

Level 1

1) 1.25 inches

$$\frac{1 \ inch \ (map)}{60 \ miles \ (real \ life)} = \frac{n}{75 \ miles}$$

Cross-multiply: 60n = 75

Divide by 60: $n = 75/60$ or $1\frac{15}{60}$ or 1.25

2) 336 girls

$$\frac{6 \ boys}{7 \ girls} = \frac{288 \ boys}{n \ girls}$$

Cross-multiply: 6n = 2016
Divide by 6:   n = 336

3) 45 feet

$$\frac{5 \ feet \ (Erica)}{2 \ feet \ (shadow)} = \frac{n \ feet \ (tree)}{18 \ feet \ (shadow)}$$

Cross-multiply: 2n = 90
Divide by 2:   n = 45

4) 3.75 hours

$$\frac{2.5 \ hours}{9000 \ seconds} = \frac{n \ hours}{13,500 \ seconds}$$

Cross-multiply: 9000n = 33,750
Divide by 9000:   n = 3.75

5) 80 feet

$$\frac{10 \ feet \ (stick)}{12 \ feet \ (shadow)} = \frac{n \ feet \ (tree)}{96 \ feet \ (shadow)}$$

Cross-multiply: 12n = 960
Divide by 12:   n = 80

Level 2

1) One penny

$$\frac{\$1,000,000\ (total\ money)}{\$100\ (charity)} = \frac{\$100\ (student's\ money)}{n\ (charity)}$$

Cross-multiply: 1,000,000n = 10,000
Divide by 1,000,000:   n = .01 dollars

2) 288 feet

$$\frac{1.5\ inches\ tall\ (preying\ mantis)}{72\ inches\ tall\ (person)} = \frac{72\ inches\ (person)}{n\ (animal)}$$

Cross-multiply: 1.5n = 5184
Divide by 1.5:   n = 3456 inches ÷ 12 = 288 feet

3) 19.5 cups of oats

$$\frac{2.5\ (cups\ of\ oats)}{25\ (cookies)} = \frac{n\ (cups\ of\ oats)}{195\ (cookies)}$$

Cross-multiply: 25n = 487.5
Divide by 25:   n = 19.5

4) 384 feet

$$\frac{\frac{1}{8}\ inch\ (flea's\ height)}{12\ inches\ (jumping\ height)} = \frac{4\ feet\ (child's\ height)}{n\ (jumping\ height)}$$

Cross-multiply: $\frac{1}{8}$n = 48

Divide by $\frac{1}{8}$:   n = 384 feet

5) 25 miles

$$\frac{3.75\ inches\ (map)}{18.75\ miles\ (real)} = \frac{5\ inches\ (map)}{n\ miles\ (real)}$$

Cross-multiply: 3.75n = 93.75
Divide by 3.75:   n = 25

Level 3

1) 121.5 years

$$\frac{50 \ hours \ (gastrotrich \ lived)}{72 \ hours \ (gastrotrich \ life-span)} = \frac{n \ years \ (giant \ tortoise)}{175 \ years \ (giant \ tortoise \ life-span)}$$

Cross-multiply: 72n = 8750
Divide by 72:   n = 121.5

2) 15 miles per hour

To answer this question, we need to find out how far a runner who completes a mile in four minutes would travel if he ran for an hour at the same speed. (We are finding speed in miles per **hour**)

$$\frac{4 \ minutes}{60 \ minutes \ in \ one \ hour} = \frac{1 \ mile}{n \ miles}$$

Cross-multiply: 4n = 60
Divide by 4:   n = 15

3) 234 feet

$$\frac{36 \ inches \ (yardstick)}{8 \ inches \ (shadow)} = \frac{n(tree)}{52 \ feet \ (shadow)}$$

Cross-multiply: 8n = 1872
Divide by 8:   n = 234

4) 106 books

$$\frac{22 \ (days)}{31 \ (days \ in \ May)} = \frac{75 \ books \ (in \ 22 \ days)}{n \ books \ (in \ May)}$$

Cross-multiply: 22n = 2325
Divide by 22:   n = 105.7

5) 1/200 of a pound

$$\frac{30,000 \ grams \ (kangaroo \ adult)}{1 \ gram \ (kangaroo \ baby)} = \frac{150 \ pounds \ (adult \ human)}{n \ pounds \ (human \ baby)}$$

Cross-multiply: 30,000n = 150
Divide by 30,000:   n = .005 or 1/200

Einstein Level

1) π/4
Pick any size square, say a 10" by 10" square. The area of that square is 100 square inches. The radius of the circle drawn within the 10" by 10" square is 5 inches.

The area of the circle $(A=\pi r^2)$ Area = 3.14 x 5 x 5 = 25π

Ratio of the areas: $\dfrac{circle}{square} = \dfrac{25\pi}{100} = \dfrac{\pi}{4}$

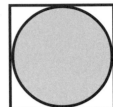

2) 16.13 miles per hour
Because we are dealing with seconds, change the time of 3 minutes and 43.13 seconds to all seconds. 3 minutes x 60 = 180 + 43.13 = 223.13 seconds

$$\frac{223.13\ seconds}{3600\ seconds\ in\ one\ hour} = \frac{1\ mile}{n\ miles}$$
Cross-multiply: 223.13n = 3600
Divide by 223.13:   n = 16.13

3) $1.22 in Canadian money

$$\frac{\$1.00\ (Canadian)}{\$.82\ (American)} = \frac{n\ (Canadian)}{\$1.00\ (American)}$$
Cross-multiply: .82n = 1
Divide by .82:   n = 1.22

4) 40.4 miles per hour

$$\frac{.621\ miles}{1\ kilometer} = \frac{n\ miles\ per\ hour}{65\ kilometers\ per\ hour}$$
Cross-multiply: n = 40.365

5) 3:00 A.M.
The ratio of normal to broken clock is 60:48 because the broken clock only goes 48 minutes during the time a normal clock goes 60 minutes.

The time we do not know is the normal clock's time when the broken clock has gone 12 hours. (12 hours is the amount of time from 12:00 noon to 12:00 midnight.)

$$\frac{60\ minutes\ (normal\ clock)}{48\ minutes\ (broken\ clock)} = \frac{n\ hours}{12\ hours}$$

Cross-multiply: 48n = 720
Divide by 48:   n = 15 hours

The normal clock started at 12:00 noon and went 15 hours: 3:00 A.M.

Super Einstein

Answer: 1019.15 feet behind

We need to first change times to seconds: Richard Webster: 276.5 seconds
                                                 Hicham El Guerrouj: 223.13 seconds

We then need to find out the distance Richard Webster would have traveled in 3 minutes and 43.13 seconds. (The time Hicham El Guerrouj crossed the finish line.)

$$\frac{5280 \; feet \; (1 \; mile)}{276.5 \; seconds \; (Webster's \; time)} = \frac{n \; feet}{223.13 \; seconds \; (Guerrouj \; crossed \; finishline)}$$

Cross-multiply: 276.5n = 1,178,126.4
Divide by 276.5:   n = 4260.85

Webster was at 4260.85 feet when Guerrouj crossed the finish line.

Webster was 5280 - 4260.85 = 1019.15 feet behind Guerrouj

Function Machines

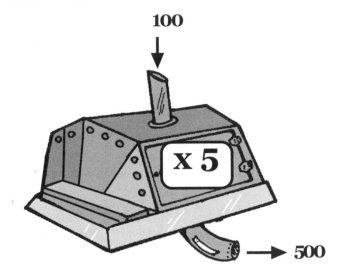

Level 1

1) Next term: 25
  100th term: 500

Machine multiplies by 5

2) Next term: 23
  150th term: 455

Because each number goes up by 3,
the first part of the function machine is x 3.

If you put a 1 into the machine, a 3 comes out.
You want an 8 to come out, so the 2nd part of
the function machine is +5.

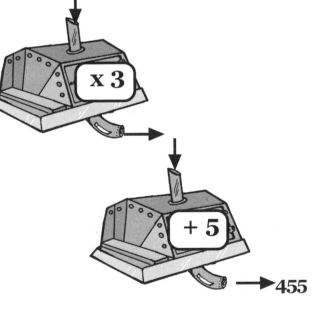

3) Next term: 28
  1000th term: 6993

The function machine is times 7
and then subtract 7.

4) Next term: 1/6
  The 89th term is 1/89

The function machine is 1 divided
by whatever number you put in.
1 ÷ n

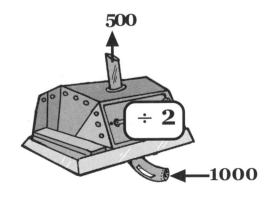

5) 500

Function machine is multiply by 2.

You must go through the function machine in reverse.
When you do, you must do the opposite operation.

Level 2

1) 75.5

Because the sequence increases by .75 each time, the first part of the function machine is multiply by .75

1 x .75 = .75 but we want 1.25, so we must add .5

2) 1002 term

The function machine is multiply by 5 and then subtract 2.

Put the number 5008 through the machine in reverse direction. Make sure you change the operations to the opposite operation when you go through the machine in reverse.

3) The next number is -1
   The 200th term is 387

Because each number goes up by 2, the function machine is multiply by 2.
1 x 2 = 2, but we want -11, so we must subtract 13.

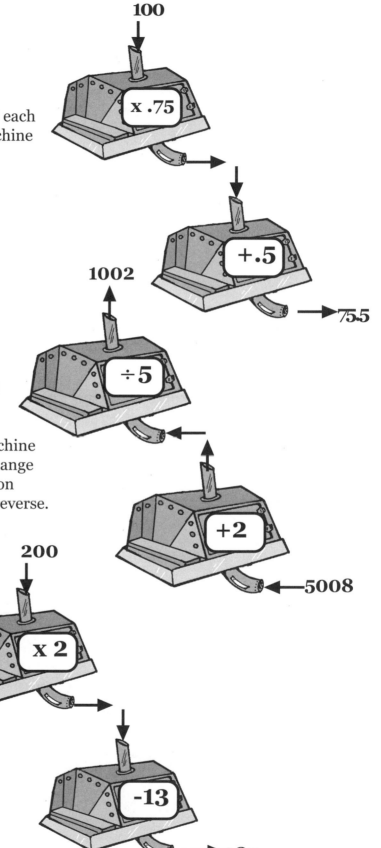

4) The next number is -50
The 100th term is -2375

The sequence loses 25 each time, so
the function machine begins with
multiply by -25.

1 x -25 = -25, but we want 100
so we must add 125.

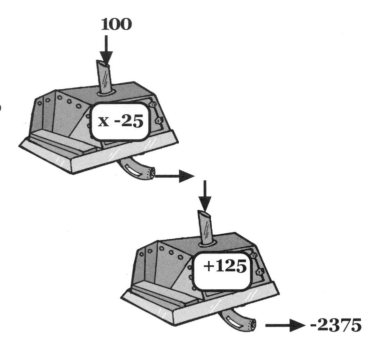

5) 211th term

The function machine is multiply
by 9 and then subtract 4.

Go through the function machine in reverse
to find the term for the number 1895. Make
sure you change the function machine operations
to the opposite operations.

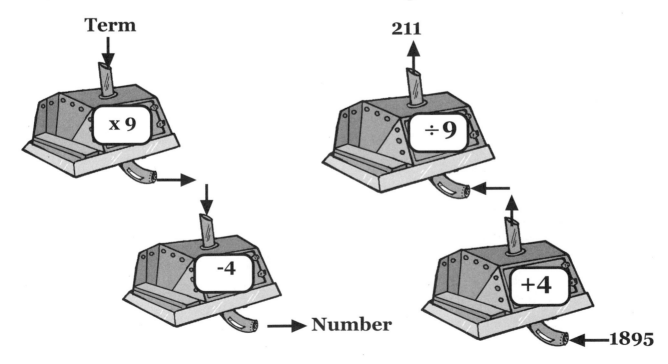

Level 3

1) The next term is 36
The 50th term is 2500

The function machine
squares the number
that enters it.

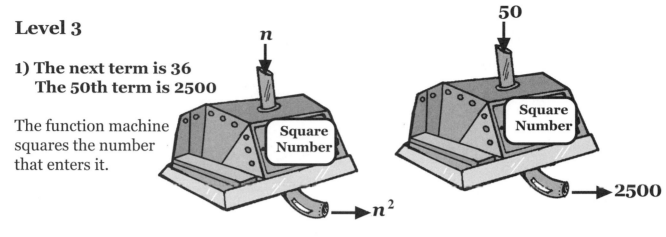

2) The next number is 31
The 500th term is 250,006

Because the sequence increases in
a way that is similar to the
"square number" sequence
(+3, +5, +7.......) we know
that n^2 must be part of the
function machine.

If we put a "1" through the n^2 machine,
a 1 comes out, but we want 7 because the
first term is a 7. The second part of our
machine is therefore +6.

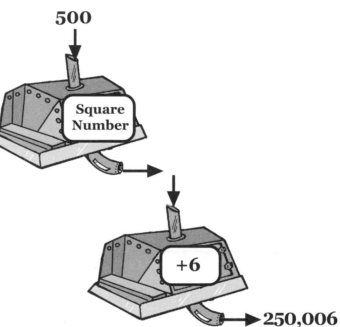

3) 1000

The function machine is cube the number that goes in. (n x n x n)

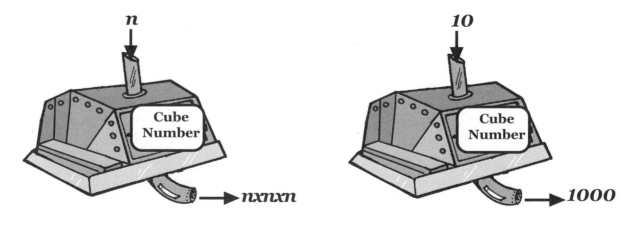

4) 10^{159}

Change numbers to exponents 10^{1} 10^{3} 10^{5}

The exponents have a sequence of 1,3,5,7

The exponents have a function machine of multiply by 2 and subtract 1. Put an 80 into the function machine and 159 comes out. The 80th term of the sequence is 10 to the 159th power.

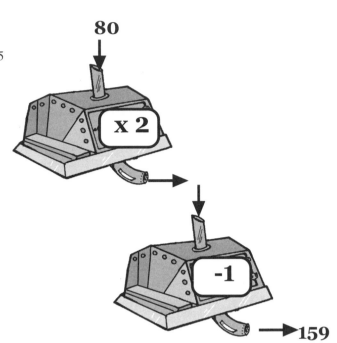

5) The number 203 is the 82nd term

The function machine starts with multiply by 2.5 because the increase is 2.5 each time. 1 x 2.5 = 2.5, but we want 1/2 so the second part of the function machine is subtract 2.

We must now put 203 through the function machine in reverse because we know the number and are looking for what term it is.

Function machine   **Reverse through the function machine**

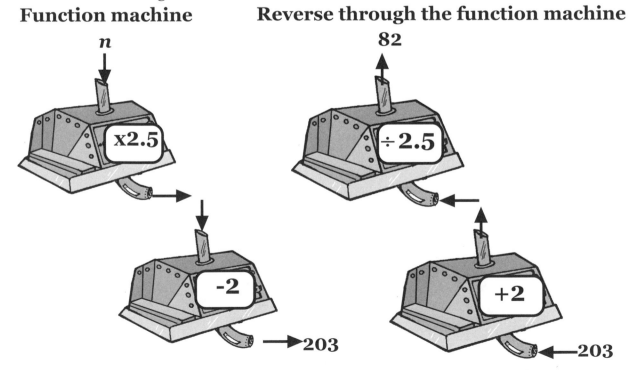

Einstein Level

1) Each denominator is the number 2 set to progressively higher powers.

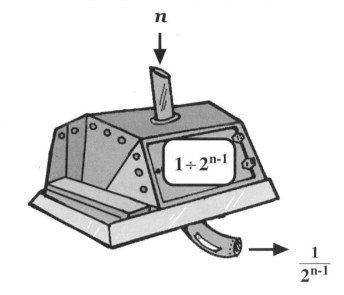

$$n$$

$$1 \div 2^{n-1}$$

$$\frac{1}{2^{n-1}}$$

2) $167,772.16

Sequence is 1,2,4,8,16

These are all powers of 2:
$2^0 \ 2^1 \ 2^2 \ 2^3$

1st term is an exponent of 0
2nd term is an exponent of 1
3rd term is an exponent of 2
4th term is an exponent of 3

To find the exponent, simply take the term and subtract 1.
25th term is $2^{25-1} = 2^{24}$

2^{24} = 16,777,216 pennies

3) See function machine at right
The numbers in the sequence are
double the previous number.
This means that there must be a
2 to some power in the function
machine.

1st term: $2^1 + 1$
2nd term: $2^2 + 2$
3rd term: $2^3 + 4$
Each term is clearly 2^n plus something.
If you look carefully, the something is 2^{n-1}

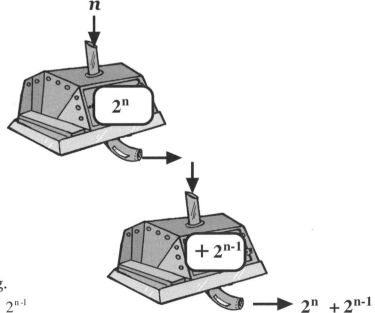

$$n$$

$$2^n$$

$$n$$

$$+ 2^{n-1}$$

$$2^n + 2^{n-1}$$

Other possible function machines include $3 \times 2^{n-1}$

4) The next number is 1/27
   The function machine:

1st term: 3^2

2nd term: 3^1

3rd term: 3^0

4th term: 3^{-1}

5th term: 3^{-2}

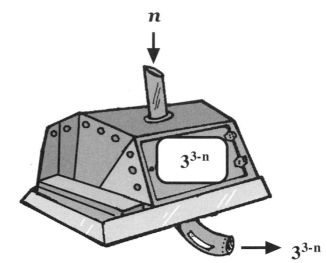

To find the exponent, simply subtract the term from 3.

Remember that negative exponents are not negative numbers. Negative exponents have you put the number under "1".
For example:

$$3^{-2} = \frac{1}{3^2} = \frac{1}{3x3} \text{ or } 1/9$$

$$3^{-3} = \frac{1}{3^3} = \frac{1}{3x3x3} \text{ or } 1/27$$

5) 1015 squares

Look for a pattern:

Number of 14 x 14 squares = 1
Number of 13 x 13 squares = 4
Number of 12 x 12 squares = 9

Pattern is now clear: 1,4,9,16.... ...
1+4+9+16+25+36................+196 = 1015

Super Einstein

Answer: : $2^{64} - 1$ dollars

1 ring: 1 move
2 rings: 3 moves
3 rings: 7 moves
4 rings: 15 moves

Sequence is clear: 1,3,7,15,   These are all powers of 2 with 1 subtracted:

1st term: $2^1 - 1$

2nd term: $2^2 - 1$

3rd term: $2^3 - 1$

4th term: $2^4 - 1$

5th term: $2^5 - 1$

64th term: $2^{64} - 1$

Don't be Fooled

Level 1

1) $5

Common wrong answer: $10

We can use algebra to solve this problem:

Language of algebra: Cat: n
                            Dog: n + 90

Equation: n + (n + 90) = 100   2n + 90 = 100   n = 5

2) 1

Common wrong answer: 10

1^{10} = 1x1x1x1x1x1x1x1x1x1=10

3) They will land at the same time.

Common wrong answer: The 50-pound bowling ball

4) 1.01

Common wrong answer: 1.00987

1.01 can also be written as 1.01000 or $1\dfrac{1000}{100,000}$

1.00987 is the same as $1\dfrac{987}{100,000}$ $1\dfrac{1000}{100,000}$ is obviously larger than $1\dfrac{987}{100,000}$

5) Both have an acceleration of zero

Common wrong answer: The car traveling at 90 miles per hour has the higher acceleration.

Acceleration concerns the change in speed. Neither car is changing speed.

Level 2

1) 200

Common wrong answer: 50

The problem is not 100 ÷ 2. The problem is 100 ÷ 1/2. This is asking how many halves will fit into 100. There are 2 halves in each whole, so there are 200 halves in 100.

2) 144 square inches

Common wrong answer: 12

There are 12 inches in a foot, but a square foot is very different than a foot. The question is asking how many 1 by 1 inch squares will fit into a 12 inch by 12 inch square. The answer is 12 x 12 = 144.

3) 1

Common wrong answer: 0

Any number to the zero power is equal to one.

4) $37.50

Common wrong answer: $25

$100 with a 50% discount is equal to $50. Now apply a 25% discount to $50. 25% of $50 is .25 x 50 = $12.50 $50 minus $12.50 = $37.50

5) 1 hour and 20 minutes

Common wrong answer: 3 hours

The answer cannot be 3 hours because Spot can paint the fence in 2 hours alone.
Spot paints 1/2 of the fence in one hour, while Steven paints 1/4 of the fence in one hour. So together, in one hour, they have painted 3/4 of the fence.

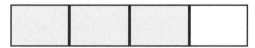

If it took them 60 minutes to paint 3/4 of the fence, then it takes them 20 minutes to paint each 1/4 of the fence. It will take them an additional 20 minutes to paint the remaining quarter. Total time 1 hour and 20 minutes.

Level 3

1) $93,750

Common wrong answer: $100,000

25% of $100,000 = .25 x 100,000 = $25,000   Warren makes $75,000 after his salary is cut 25%.

Warren's boss will now give Warren a 25% raise to his $75,000 salary.

Raise: .25 x 75,000 = $18,750   Warren's new salary: $75,000 plus the raise of $18,750 = $93,750

2) 1728 cubic inches

Common wrong answer: 12 or 144

Volume is found by multiplying length times width times height. A cubic foot is 12 inches by 12 inches by 12 inches = 1728 cubic inches.

In other words, there are 1728 1" by 1" by 1" cubes inside a one foot cube.

3) 10^{31}

Common wrong answer: 100^{30} or 10^{300}

Each increase in the exponent makes the number ten times larger.

4) $50

Common wrong answer: $5,000

.5% is not the same as 50%.   .5% is half of 1% or 1/2%

1% of $10,000 is 100 so 1/2% is only $50

5) $108

Common wrong answer: $12

There are 3 x 3 x 3 = 27 cubic feet in each cubic yard.

27 x $4 = $108

Einstein Level

1) 44.44 miles per gallon

Common wrong answer: 45 miles per gallon

Miles per gallon of gas is easy to find------Miles driven are divided by the number of gallons used. We need to find out how much gas Jessica used on her round trip to school and back.

Gas used on the way to school: 50 miles each gallon and a 10 mile drive: Jessica used 1/5 of a gallon of gas.

Gas used on the trip home: 40 miles each gallon and a 10 mile drive: Jessica used 1/4 of a gallon of gas.

Total gallons: 1/4 + 1/5 = 9/20 of a gallon

20 miles driven ÷ 9/20 gallon of gas = 44.44 miles per gallon

2) 40 miles per hour

Common wrong answer: 45 mph

Remember that Distance (in miles) = Speed x Time (in hours)
Distance: 20 miles
Average speed: n
Time: There are two different trips that Adam took.
Trip to school: Because his speed was 60 miles in 60 minutes (60 mph), it must have taken Adam 10 minutes to go the 10 miles.

Trip home: Because his speed was 30 miles in 60 minutes (30 mph), it must have taken Adam 20 minutes to go the 10 miles.

Total time: 10 minutes + 20 minutes = 30 minutes or .5 hour

Equation: Distance = Speed x Time   20 miles = Speed x .5 hour
                                          20 miles = n x .5

Divide both sides of the equation by .5   n = 40 mph

3) 10 trillion universes

Common wrong answer: I do not have a clue as to what you are talking about.

There are 10^{100} zeros in the number googolplex, but only 10^{87} atoms in the entire universe.

$\dfrac{10^{100}}{10^{87}} = 10^{13} = 10,000,000,000,000$ times as many zeros in googolplex

as there are atoms in the universe.

4) 7.06 miles per hour

Make up a distance for the trip to school that can easily be divided by 12 and 5. (We will use 60, but any number is fine, the answer will end up the same.)

Trip to school: 5 hours   (60 miles ÷ 12 miles per hour)
Trip home: 12 hours   (60 miles ÷ 5 miles per hour)
Entire trip: Distance = Speed x Time   120 = Average speed x 17
                                                 Average speed: 120 ÷ 17 = 7.06 mph

5) Choice #2

Common wrong answer: Choice #1
Let's look at the amount of allowance Esteban would be paid for each choice.
Choice #1:   First 4 weeks------$100
              5th - 8th week-----$110
              9th - 12th week----$120
              Total for the first 12 weeks---$330

Choice #2   1st week------$25
             2nd week-----$26.50
             3rd week-----$28.00
             4th week-----$29.50
             5th week-----$31.00
             6th week-----$32.50
             7th week-----$34.00
             8th week-----$35.50
             9th week-----$37.00
             10th week----$38.50
             11th week----$40.00
             12th week----$41.50
             Total for the first 12 weeks----$399.00

It is hard to believe that choice #2 would be the better choice, but most people do not take into account the fact that the raises are added to previous raises and that a $1.50 raise per week is not the same as a $6 per four weeks raise.

Super Einstein

Answer: 2/3

Common wrong answer 1/2

There are two different ways to help your
brain understand the correct answer.

#1:   Ask yourself the following question:

What is the probability that the knight would pick a box with similar frogs in it? (Both
truthtellers or both liars) The answer of course is 2/3.

Another way to look at the situation is that you are holding one of the following boxes:

If you are holding frog A, then frog B is going to be a truthteller.
If you are holding frog B, then frog A is going to be a truthteller.
If you are holding frog C, then frog D is going to be a liar.

Three situations, two have the remaining frog telling the truth. 2/3

Eccentric Mathematician

Contest 1

Bottom Step) There is no way to tell
If n is negative, 2n will be smaller than n.
If n is 0, they are the same.

2) There is no way to tell
If n is a fraction smaller than 1, then n^2 will be smaller than n.
If n is one, n and n^2 will both be equal to one.

3) Left side is larger
The left side is always one larger than the right side.

4) They are the same

$$\frac{25}{100} \times n = \frac{25n}{100} \qquad\qquad \frac{n}{100} \times 25 = \frac{25n}{100}$$

Top Step) Left side is larger
The left side is always 7 larger than the right side.

Contest 2

Bottom Step) The left side is larger
If n is positive, then n÷5 is always larger than n÷6.

2) The left side is larger.
100÷6 = 16.67   101÷7 = 14.43

3) There is no way to tell
If n is a negative number, then 3n is smaller than 2n. If n = 0, they are the same.

4) Left side is larger

Top Step) There is no way to tell
If n is a negative number, then n÷5 is smaller than n÷6. If n = 0, then they are the same.

Contest 3

Bottom Step) There is no way to tell
If n = 1, they are the same.

2) There is no way to tell
n° may equal 90° or it may equal 91°. There is no way to tell.

3) There is no way to tell
y must equal 4 or -4.   x must equal 4 or -8

4) Right side is larger
The longest side of a triangle can never exceed the combined lengths of the other two sides.

Top Step) Left side is larger
The circumference of the circle is equal to 3.14 diameters. Lengths 1 + 2 + 3 = 3 diameters.

Contest 4

Bottom Step) The left side is larger
Circumference divided by the diameter is equal to pi. (3.14)

2) The right side is larger.
Because n is negative, the left side is always negative while the right side is always positive.

3) There is no way to tell

If x is a negative number, then x is smaller than $\frac{1}{2}$x. If n = 0, they are the same.

4) There is no way to tell
The left side is always positive. The right side is always positive. If n is equal to -1, then both sides are equal. (- -1 = 1 and -1 x -1 = 1)

Top Step) There is no way to tell
x and y could be equal to 5 and 12 or they can be equal to -5 and -12.

Contest 5

Bottom Step) They are the same
They are both equal to 1.

2) Right side is larger
The interior angles of a triangle add up to 180 degrees.

3) They are the same
Because n + x = 180 degrees, then x must equal 180 - n.

4) Right side is larger
There are 18 gallons left in the tank. The cost would be $36.

Top Step) Right side is larger
8n + 9 = 4n + 3   Solving equation: 4n = -6   n = -1.5

Contest 6

Bottom Step) There is no way to tell
If A, B, C, and D are all zero, then both sides are equal.
If they are all equal to 1, then 1 + 1 + 1 + 1 = 4 and 1 x 1 x 1 x 1 = 1

2) The left side is larger

3) The left side is larger
Because n is a negative number, n is always larger than 2n.

4) The right side is larger
The left side is always negative. The right side is always positive.

Top Step) Left side is larger
In a parallelogram, the area is largest when the parallelogram is a rectangle. As the parallelogram gets "squashed", its area decreases.

Permutations

Level 1

1) 6

$_3P_3$ Three errands taken three at a time: $3! = 3 \times 2 \times 1 = 6$

2) 24

$_4P_4$ Four numbers taken four at a time: $4! = 4 \times 3 \times 2 \times 1 = 24$

3) 120 ways

$_5P_5$ Five players taken five at a time: $5! = 5 \times 4 \times 3 \times 2 \times 1 = 120$

4) 5040

$_7P_7$ Seven letters taken seven at a time: $7! = 7 \times 6 \times 5 \times 4 \times 3 \times 2 \times 1 = 5040$

5) 362,880

$_9P_9$ Nine players taken nine at a time:

$$9! = 9 \times 8 \times 7 \times 6 \times 5 \times 4 \times 3 \times 2 \times 1 = 362,880$$

Level 2

1) 90

$_{10}P_2$ 10 people taken 2 at a time: $\boxed{10 \times 9}$ x 8 x 7 x 6 x 5 x 4 x 3 x 2 x 1

2) The same number of ways

Jay: $_5P_4$ 5 paintings 4 at a time: $\boxed{5 \times 4 \times 3 \times 2}$ x 1

5 x 4 x 3 x 2 = 120 ways

Nancy: $_5P_5$ 5 paintings 5 at a time: 5 x 4 x 3 x 2 x 1 = 120 ways

3) 20,160 ways

$_8P_6$ 8 paintings taken 6 at a time: $\boxed{8 \times 7 \times 6 \times 5 \times 4 \times 3}$ x 2 x 1

8 x 7 x 6 x 5 x 4 x 3 = 20,160

4) 4

$_4P_3$ 4 books taken 3 at a time: $\boxed{4 \times 3 \; \times 2}$ x 1

4 x 3 x 2 = 24

Eliminate groups that are the same except for order.
     To do this divide by $_3P_3$ 3 taken 3 at a time: 3 x 2 x 1 = 6   24 ÷ 6 = 4

5) 479,001,600

$_{12}P_{12}$ 12 taken 12 at a time:

12 x 11 x 10 x 9 x 8 x 7 x 6 x 5 x 4 x 3 x 2 x 1 = 479,001,600

Level 3

1) 230,300

$_{50}P_4$ 50 students taken 4 at a time: $\boxed{50 \times 49 \times 48 \times 47}$ .... = 5,527,200

Now we need to eliminate the quartets that are the same except for order.
Divide by $_4P_4$ = 4 x 3 x 2 x 1 = 24   5,527,200 ÷ 24 = 230,300

2) 9:00 A.M. the next morning

$_7P_7$ Seven objects taken 7 at a time: 7 x 6 x 5 x 4 x 3 x 2 x 1 = 5040

5040 permutations ÷ 4 per minute = 1260 minutes.

1260 ÷ 60 = 21 hours   Starting at 12:00 noon and adding 21 hours
                               equals 9:00 A.M. the next day.

3) 56 combinations of three people

$_8P_3$ Eight people taken 3 at a time: $\boxed{8 \times 7 \times 6}$ x 5 x 4 x 3 x 2 x 1 = 336

Now we need to eliminate the groups of three that are the same except for order.
Divide by $_3P_3$ 3 x 2 x 1 = 6   336 ÷ 6 = 56

4) 1287 combinations

$_{13}P_5$ 13 players taken 5 at a time:
                $\boxed{13 \times 12 \times 11 \times 10 \times 9}$ x 8 x 7 x 6 x 5 x 4 x 3 x 2 x 1 = 154,440

Now we need to eliminate the players who are the same except for order.
To do this, divide by $_5P_5$ 5 x 4 x 3 x 2 x 1 = 120   154,440 ÷ 120 = 1287

5) 4950
$_{100}P_2$ 100 people taken two at a time: $\boxed{100 \times 99}$ x 98 x 97............= 9900

Now we need to eliminate the pairs that are the same.
(**A** shaking **B** is the same as **B** shaking **A**)   Divide by $_2P_2$ 2 x 1 = 2

9900 ÷ 2 = 4950

Einstein Level

1) 10,000 seconds

Start with 0000, then keep counting 0001, 0002,0003.........................9999
>   These combinations are numbers that start with 0000 and count until you get to
>   9,999. There are 10,000 numbers when you count from 0 to 9,999.

2) During 8th grade

$_{15}P_4$ 15 charms taken 4 at a time: $\boxed{15 \times 14 \times 13 \times 12}$ x 11 x 10.................= 32,760

Eliminate all groups that are the same except for order.
To do this, divide by $_4P_4$ = 4 x 3 x 2 x 1 = 24   32,760 ÷ 24 = 1365 different combinations

1365 ÷ 180 days in a school year = 7.58 years
Lindsey will have enough combinations for about 7.5 years. She will run out of
combinations during her 8th grade year.

3) 1,998,000

$_{1000}P_2$ 1000 people taken 2 at a time: $\boxed{1000 \times 999}$ x 998 x 997......... = 999,000

Eliminate pairs that are the same:
Divide by $_2P_2$ 2 x 1 = 2   999,000 ÷ 2 = 499,500 different pairs

Each group of two will perform exactly 4 handshakes: (Tom will use his right hand to shake
Dave's right hand and then Dave's left hand. Tom will then use his left hand to shake Dave's
right hand and then Dave's left hand.) 499,500 x 4 = 1,998,000

4) 9 paintings

365 days x 41 years = 14,965 days + about 10 leap days = 14,975 days

She will need $_?P_5$ This is some number of permutations taken 5 at a time and
                must equal at least 14,965. $\boxed{9 \times 8 \times 7 \times 6 \times 5}$ x 4 x 3 x 2 x 1 = 15,120

The eccentric mathematician must buy at least 9 paintings.

5) 2,594,592,000

You first need to find the number of permutations of 15 players taken 8 at a time. (Every possible permutation of the team without the pitchers added.)

$_{15}P_8$ 15 players taken 8 at a time:

15 x 14 x 13 x 12 x 11 x 10 x 9 x 8 x 7 x 6 x 5 x 4 x 3 x 2 x 1.......= 259,459,200

Each one of the 259,459,200 permutations has 10 different possibilities for the 9th player in the batting order.   259,459,200 x 10 = 2,594,592,000

Super Einstein

Answer: February 1st at noon

Instead of thinking that you must match 7 spheres with 9 holes (Which is very confusing), try thinking of 9 holes that can only be taken 7 at a time because there are only 7 spheres.

$_9P_7$ 9 holes taken 7 at a time: $\boxed{9 \times 8 \times 7 \times 6 \times 5 \times 4 \times 3}$ x 2 x 1 = 181,440 permutations

181,440 ÷ 4 per minute = 45,360 minutes

45,360 minutes ÷ 60 = 756 hours

756 hours ÷ 24 = 31.5 days

31 days would be 12:00 A.M. midnight on February 1st.

31.5 days would be noon on February 1st.

Understanding Bases

Level 1

1) 49 rocks

This 1 in base 7 means one group of 49.
     0 groups of 7
         0 groups of one

2) Yes

The number 3 in base 7 is the same in base 10. In both cases it means 3 ones.

3) 236 pounds

2 groups of 49 can be taken from 125 with 27 left over.
     3 groups of 7 can be taken from 27 with 6 left over for the one's column.

2401	343	49	7	1
		2	3	6

4) 7 fingers

We have 10 fingers and base 10. It would be reasonable to think that Septonians have 7 fingers.

5) 202

2 groups of 49 can be taken from 100 with 2 left over.
     0 groups of 7 can be taken from the 2, so 2 is left over.
         2 in the one's column

2401	343	49	7	1
		2	0	2

Level 2

1)

In base 2 each column is found by multiplying by 2. (Remember in base 10 each column is found by multiplying by 10)

256	128	64	32	16	8	4	2	1

2) 11001

1 group of 16 can be taken from 25 with 9 left over.

    1 group of 8 can be taken from 9 with 1 left over.

        0 groups of 4

           0 groups of 2

              1 left over for the one's column.

256	128	64	32	16	8	4	2	1
				1	1	0	0	1

3) 8

1000 in base 2 means one group of 8 and 0 groups of 4,2, and 1.

256	128	64	32	16	8	4	2	1
					1	0	0	0

4) Multiply by 5 to find each column.

390,625	78,125	15,625	3125	625	125	25	5	1

5) 400

There are 4 groups of 25 in 100 base 10.

390,625	78,125	15,625	3125	625	125	25	5	1
						4	0	0

Level 3

1) 117,649

		117,649	16,807	2401	343	49	7	1
		1	**0**	**0**	**0**	**0**	**0**	**0**

2) $64
1 group of 64

256	128	64	32	16	8	4	2	1
		1	**0**	**0**	**0**	**0**	**0**	**0**

3) 1/7

16,807	2401	343	49	7	1	1/7	1/49	1/343
		0	**0**	**0**	**0•**	**1**		

Base 7 columns

		1000	100	10	1	1/10	1/100	1/1000
					•			

Base 10 columns

4) 14 + 5 + 1/7 + 2/49

Base 7   25.12 means: 2 groups of 7
                                   5 groups of 1
                                   1 group of 1/7
                                   2 groups of 1/49

5) The Septon ate more

The Septon ate 5 groups of 1/7   or   5/7
The American ate 5 groups of 1/10   or   5/10 or 1/2 of the cookie.

Einstein Level

1) 1

32	16	8	4	2	1	1/2	1/4	1/8
		0	0	0	0.	1	1	1

Base 2   .111111 means-----------1/2 + 1/4 + 1/8 + 1/16 This approaches 1

2) 11,333,311

823,543	117,649	16,807	2401	343	49	7	1
1	1	3	3	3	3	1	1

1 group of 823,543 in 1,000,000 with 176,457 left over.

1 group of 117,649 in the 176,457 with 58,808 left over.

3 groups of 16,807 in the 58,808 with 8387 left over.

3 groups of 2401 in 8387 with 1184 left over.

3 groups of 343 in 1184 with 155 left over.

3 groups of 49 in 155 with 8888 left over.

1 group of 7 in 8 with 1 left over.

1 in the one's column.

3) $133\dfrac{181}{343}$

2 groups of 49 = 98

  5 groups of 7 = 35

    0 ones

      3 groups of 1/7 = 3/7

        4 groups of 1/49 = 4/49

          6 groups of 1/343 = 6/343

16807	2401	343	49	7	1	1/7	1/49	1/343	
			2	**5**	**0.**	**3**	**4**	**6**	Base 7 columns

98 + 35 + 3/7 + 4/49 + 6/343 = $133\dfrac{181}{343}$

4) 10

1 group of 13

5) 5&*

5 groups of 169 in 1000 with 155 remaining.

  11 groups of 13 in 155 with 12 left over. (Remember that 11 in base 13 is the digit &.)

    12 ones which is written with the digit * in base 13.

Base 13

28,561	2197	169	13	1
		5	**&**	**#**

Super Einstein

Answer: 2181 days

Base 13

28,561	2197	169	13	1
		*	&	#

means 10
  10 groups of 1 = 10

& means 11
  11 groups of 13 = 143

* means 12
  12 groups of 169 = 2028

2028 + 143 + 10 = 2181

Who Wants to be a Googolillionaire?

Answers

$Million   What is $33\frac{1}{3}$% of 9?   **3**

$Billion   What is the formula for the area of a circle? $\pi\mathbf{r}^2$

$Trillion   What is the formula for the circumference of a circle? $\pi\mathbf{D}$

$Quadrillion   How many millimeters are in a meter?   **1000**

$Quintillion   How many square feet are in a square yard?   **9**

$Sextillion   What is the weight of a liter of water expressed in kilograms?   **1**

$Septillion   Change 1/9 to a decimal.   **.11111**

$Octillion   A 3-foot stick casts a shadow of 8 feet. If at the same time a tree casts a shadow of 15 feet, how tall is the tree? $\mathbf{5\frac{5}{8}}$

$Nonillion   What is the formula for the volume of a cylinder? $\pi\mathbf{r}^2 \mathbf{x\ h}$

$Decillion   If Distance equals Speed times Time (D=SxT), then what does time equal in terms of speed and distance?   **D÷S**

$Undecillion   A metal block is made of nickel and copper. The weight of the metals in the block are in a ratio of 2:9. The weight of the block is 407 pounds. What is the weight of the nickel?   **74 pounds**

$Duodecillion   A right triangle has legs of 9 feet and 12 feet. How long is the hypotenuse?   **15 feet**

$Tredecillion   The tax in a state is 5%. If Eric paid $4.60 tax for a bike, what was the cost of the bike before sales tax was added?   **$92**

$Quattuordecillion   What is the weight of a cubic meter of water? Express your answer in kilograms.   **1 kilogram per cubic decimeter and 1000 cubic decimeters in cubic meter: 1000 kilograms**

$Googol   How many microns are in a meter?   **1,000,000**

Who Wants to be a Googolillionaire?

Answers

$Million   Write .02 as a percent.   **2%**

$Billion   Write 7% as a decimal. **.07**

$Trillion   What is 65% of 200?   **130**

$Quadrillion   A book is discounted 45%. If the original price is $40, what is the new price?   **$22**

$Quintillion   1/3 + 1/7 =   **10/21**

$Sextillion $6\frac{1}{8} x \frac{1}{7} =$ **7/8**

$Septillion   A book cost $8.50 without tax. If the tax rate is 7%, what is the total cost of the book including tax?   **$9.10**

$Octillion $18 - 6\frac{1}{9} =$ $11\frac{8}{9}$

$Nonillion $22\frac{1}{2} \div \frac{1}{8} =$ **180**

$Decillion   A triangle has an area of 60 square inches and a base of 10 inches. What is its height?   **12 inches**

$Undecillion   Compare a decimeter to a meter using percents. (A decimeter is what percent of a meter?)   **10%**

$Duodecillion   Compare a gallon to a quart using percents. (A gallon is what percent of a quart?)   **400%**

$Tredecillion   What is the Least Common Multiple of 3,4,5?   **60**

$Quattuordecillion   When a circle's radius triples, what happens to its area?   **x9**

$Googol   A store sells books for 50% off on Sundays. The store advertises that on Easter Sunday the store takes an additional 25% off. What would a pile of books cost on Easter Sunday that normally sell for $100 on a Thursday?   **$37.50**

Math Contests Level 1
Answers

1) 15n

$15 for each cat times n cats = 15n dollars

2) 2 inches

1/2 inch for every 3/4 mile. There are four 3/4 mile sections in 3 miles, therefore there must be four 1/2 inch sections on the map.

3) 10 students

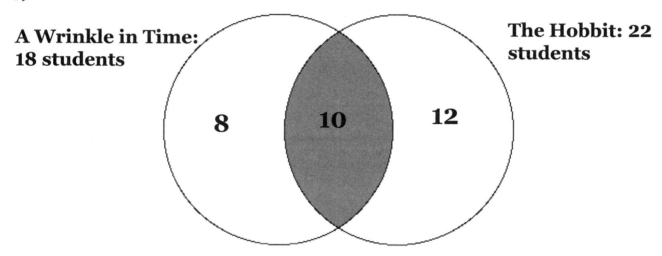

A Wrinkle in Time: 18 students

The Hobbit: 22 students

8   10   12

4) 5/6

The probability of a "5" is 1/6.   The probability the number will not be a "5" is 1 - 1/6 = 5/6

5) 120 permutations

5! = 5 x 4 x 3 x 2 x 1 = 120

Math Contests Level 2
Answers

1) 59 minutes

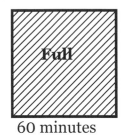

Full

60 minutes

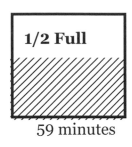

1/2 Full

59 minutes

1/4 Full

58 minutes

2) 50 miles per gallon

10-2 method: Change to 10 miles with 2 gallons of gas. The way to solve this problem is clearly $10 \div 2 = 5$ miles per gallon.

Real problem: $481.25 \div 9.625 = 50$ miles per gallon

3) 23.1 gallons

Ratios:

$$\frac{3.5 \ gallons}{985 \ (area \ of \ wall)} = \frac{n \ gallons}{6501 \ (area \ of \ wall)}$$

What did you multiply 985 by to get 6501? $6501 \div 985 = 6.6$

$$\frac{3.5 \ gallons \ x \ 6.6}{985 \ (area \ of \ wall) \ x \ 6.6} = \frac{23.1 \ gallons}{6501 \ (area \ of \ wall)}$$

Another method: Cross-multiply: $985n = 22{,}753.5$ $n = 23.1$

4) 85°

The sum of the interior angles of a triangle is 180°. 180-10=170° for the two n's. Each n must therefore equal $170 \div 2 = 85°$

5) 11 posts

Common wrong answer: 10 posts

Math Contests Level 3
Answers

1) Bill has more money.

10^{10} is ten times larger than 10^9

2) $960

Cost of computer: n
Sales tax: 7% of n or .07n

Equation: .07n = 67.20

Divide both sides by .07: n = $960

3) x/n gallons

2-10 method: Nancy's car gets 2 miles per gallon. If she traveled 10 miles, how many gallons of gas did she use?

2-10 problem: It is fairly obvious that she used 10÷2 = 5 gallons of gas.

Real problem: Place letters back into the problem   x÷n gallons   x/n gallons

4) $246

$1080 divided by 360° = $3 for each degree of the circle. Car payment + college loan + food = 278 degrees.   The miscellaneous expenses must equal 360 - 278 = 82°

82° x $3 = $246

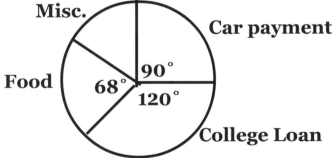

5) 12 inches

The shaded part is 1/8 of the entire square,
so the area of the square is 18 x 8 = 144 square inches.

If the area of the square is 144 square inches,
each side of the square must be 12 inches.

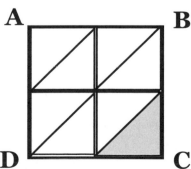

Math Contests Einstein Level
Answers (Test 1)

1) 10 feet

The radius of the circle can be found because we know the area. $A = \pi\, r^2$

$314 = 3.14 \times r^2$

Divide both sides by 3.14 $100 = r^2$ $r = 10$

BD is the radius of the circle and a diagonal of the square. The other diagonal is AC. AC is equal in length to BD which is 10 feet.

2) 5%

80% New York Times   50% U.S.A. Today

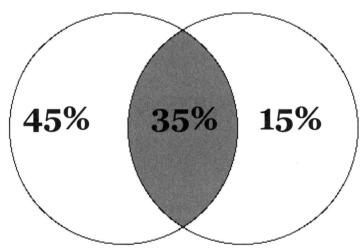

$45\% + 35\% + 15\% = 95\%$ 5% remaining

3) 1700 square feet

Together, Anna, Eric and Meadow painted $1/6 + 1/5 + 1/4 = 37/60$ of the wall.

The remaining part is 23/60 and also 3910 square feet.
Find 1/60 by dividing 3910 by 23: $3910 \div 23 = 170$ square feet for each 1/60

Anna painted 1/6 or 10/60
Each 1/60 = 170 square feet
$10/60 = 170 \times 10 = 1700$ square feet

Math Contests Einstein Level
Answers (Test 1)

4) $91

Pick any diameter for the circle, say 10 feet.
The area of the circle is 3.14 x 5 x 5 = 78.5

The area of the square can be found by dividing it
into two triangles. The base is the diameter and
the height is half the diameter.

The area of each triangle is 25 square feet, so the
area of the square is 50 square feet.

The area of the circle (78.5) - Area
of the square (50) = 28.5 square feet

28.5 ÷ 4 = 7.125 is the area of
the savings section.

Fraction for savings section:

$$\frac{7.125}{78.5} = .0908 \text{ x } \$1000 = \$90.80$$

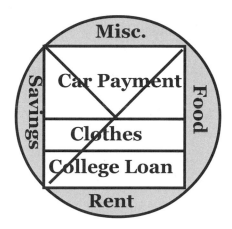

5) $\frac{1}{2}n$ **pages in** *n* **minutes**

Martha reads 300 pages in 10 hours.

Because there are 60 minutes in an hour, Martha reads 300 pages in 600 minutes.

300 pages in 600 minutes is a rate of 1/2 page per minute.

If Martha reads 1/2 page per minute, she will be able to read $\frac{1}{2}$n pages in *n* minutes.

Math Contests Einstein Level
Answers (Test 2)

1) 27 feet

The triangle is an isosceles triangle so the left angle must also be 60°. Because there are 180 degrees in a triangle, the remaining angle must also be 60°. If all three angles are the same, the triangle must be an equilateral triangle.

2) $800 + xyn dollars

Use 2-10-100 method:

Class of 100 students (n)
Each work: 2 more hours (x)
Pay: 10 dollars per hour (y)

2-10 method: Now it is easy to see that each student will earn 2 x 10 = $20
Real problem: Each student earns xy dollars

2-10 problem: If each student earns $20 and there are 100 students, they will all earn 20 x 100 = $2000
Real problem: n students each earn xy dollars. They will all earn a total of xy times n or xyn dollars of additional money.

3) 1728 xyh

The volume is x times y times h = xyh cubic feet
    There are 1728 cubic inches in each cubic foot. (12 x 12 x 12 = 1728)

The volume is xyh cubic feet and there are 1728 cubic inches in each cubic foot. The volume expressed in cubic inches is: 1728 times xyh cubic inches.

4) 19.625 square inches

Area of large circle: 3.14 x 5 x 5 = 78.5 square inches
Area of half the large circle: 78.5 ÷ 2 = 39.25 square inches
    Area of the small circle: (radius is 2.5 inches)
        3.14 x 2.5 x 2.5 = 19.625 square inches.
            Area of half of the large circle (39.25) minus
            area of the small circle = 19.625 square inches.

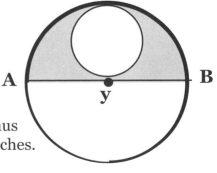

5) .75n

A shirt that cost n dollars and is marked up 50% sells for 1.5n. Employees can buy the shirt for 1/2 price----.75n.

Math Contests Super Einstein Level
Answers

1) 4 minutes and 57 seconds

When the race was done, George had completed 5280 - 480 = 4800 feet.

$$\frac{4800\ feet\ (George's\ distance)}{4.5\ minutes\ (George's\ time)} = \frac{5280\ (Full\ mile)}{n\ (George's\ time\ for\ a\ mile)}$$

What did you multiply 4800 by to get 5280? 5280÷4800 = 1.1

$$\frac{4800\ x\ 1.1\ feet\ (George's\ distance)}{4.5\ x\ 1.1\ minutes\ (George's\ time)} = \frac{5280\ (Full\ mile)}{4.95\ (George's\ time\ for\ a\ mile)}$$

.95 minutes is equal to how many seconds?

.95 x 60 = 57 seconds

2) 15/34

The probability that the first card is not a heart is 3/4. If the first is not a heart, then the probability that the second card is not a heart is 38/51. (This is because there are 38 non-heart cards left and a total of 51 cards left.)

The probability that both cards are not hearts is therefore 3/4 x 38/51 = $\frac{114}{204}$. Now we know that the probability of at least one being hearts is

$1 - \frac{114}{204} = \frac{204}{204} - \frac{114}{204} = \frac{90}{204}$ which reduces to 15/34.

3) $\frac{n-1}{n}$**x 100** $= \frac{100(n-1)}{n}$

The fraction of the food left is $\frac{n-1}{n}$. To change a fraction or decimal to a percent, simply

multiply by 100. $\frac{n-1}{n}\ x\ 100\ =\ \frac{100(n-1)}{n}$

Math Contests Super Einstein Level
Answers

4) 50.49 cubic inches

The volume of each ball is $1.33 \times 3.14 \times 2^3 = 33.41$ cubic inches.
The volume of the three tennis balls is 100.23 cubic inches.
The volume of the cylinder is area of circle times height =
$3.14 \times 2 \times 2 \times 12 = 150.72$ cubic inches.

Volume of remaining space is $150.72 - 100.23 = 50.49$ cubic inches.